When Flesh
Begins To Creep

When Flesh Begins To Creep

JUDITH GOROG

LONDON
VICTOR GOLLANCZ LTD
1986

First published in the U.S.A. 1982
as *A Taste For Quiet*
by Philomel Books,
a division of The Putnam Publishing Group

First published in Great Britain 1986
by Victor Gollancz Ltd,
14 Henrietta Street, London WC2E 8QJ

British Library Cataloguing in Publication Data

Gorog, Judith
[A taste for quiet and other disquieting tales].
When flesh begins to creep.
I. [A taste for quiet and other disquieting
tales]   II. Title
813'.54[J]

ISBN 0-575-03797-0

Printed in Great Britain by
St Edmundsbury Press, Bury St Edmunds, Suffolk

For Sallie, Ruth, and Tasha,
and especially for István.

CONTENTS

A Story About Death

It was a Tuesday morning in spring when Death walked in our kitchen door. Mama was taking cookies out of the oven. I was sitting on the floor of the pantry, in my special place, drawing and feeling a little sad. Mama was annoyed with me for leaving my baby brother asleep on the big bed in the playroom. He was lying in the middle of the bed with our stuffed animals around him and a big pile of clean laundry at the foot of the bed. He couldn't roll off, but Mama says we might forget he is there in the middle of that mess, and do a somersault on him. True, my sister and I usually do somersaults on that bed.

Death didn't even knock. The door opened and I smelled a basement smell and felt cold air all around me. He didn't see me. He just looked at the cookies on the table and at the cake Mama had just frosted. He looked and looked at that cake. I looked and looked at him. He was just like the pictures of him in books: yellowish-white bones in a long brown robe. The hood was pulled up so that you could hardly see his head. He looked up from the cake at Mama.

"I've come for one of your children. You have three." He held up his bony fingers and counted, "One seven-year-old, one five-year-old, and one baby two months old. Which will it be?"

Mama stopped taking cookies off the baking sheet. She didn't even look scared. "Must it be one of the children? How about me?"

"How about me!" mimicked Death in a high, mean voice. "Aw. You parents are all the same. No. I have my orders. It must be a child, by twelve noon, so make up your mind. I'm late."

Mama didn't answer him. Was she mad enough to give me to him? I wanted to run to her, but I stayed very still, like a little animal in the forest. I made myself as small as I could and waited to hear what Mama would say. But Mama still didn't answer, just poured a mug of tea for Death and then one for herself. She passed a plate of cookies to Death, then took a sip of her tea. Death ate six cookies in a flash. I have never seen anyone so greedy. Mama poured some milk into her tea. She drank slowly, with a serious face. I could hardly sit still. Death helped himself to another six cookies.

The kitchen clock hummed. Death crunched his cookies and slurped his tea. Finally Mama said, very slowly, with sips of tea in between, "I have read somewhere that you like games."

"No. No. No games. Those days are over."

"And must it be today?" continued Mama, as if Death had not interrupted her.

"Well," said Death, with a mouth full of cookie. "I must do my job by noon."

Mama got a big knife and cut a large slice of cake, put it on a plate, and got out a fork. Then she offered the plate of cake to Death.

Taking the plate, Death said, "If I don't get one today, I have two more chances."

Mama looked interested. "The children are so young. If you don't get one now, then all of them get to grow very old, to be truly ready for you?"

"Well, yes. I get three tries this time. But I won't miss. No tricks. I'm watching the clock. Well. Which one?" He mumbled because his mouth was full of cake.

Mama took a deep breath. "I'm thinking."

The clock said one minute to twelve.

"Hurry, woman!" gasped Death, nearly choking on his cake. The plate clattered to the kitchen table. As he stood up, all kinds of crumbs fell from his robe to the kitchen floor.

"I suppose it must be the baby," whispered Mama. Her back was to me and I saw that she had her fingers crossed behind her back as she spoke. I nearly cried out.

Death raced upstairs. "He's not in his bed!" he yelled.

"Oh," said Mama. "Where can he be?"

She looked at me and put her finger to her lips, then got out the broom and began to sweep up the crumbs.

Death raced downstairs and out the front door to look in the baby carriage under the cherry tree. It was empty. Then he looked in the baby's bouncy chair.

Twelve was striking on the church clock. I counted under my breath. Eleven. Twelve.

Death slammed out of the kitchen door. "I'll be back tomorrow," he called over his shoulder, and was gone.

Mama and I raced upstairs. The baby was safe, asleep under a large fuzzy bear, the one I've slept with since I was two.

"Mama, what will you do?" I asked.

Mama gave me a big hug. "I'm thinking. With the baby it may just be possible to trick him two more times."

All afternoon Mama was very quiet. She made me promise not to tell what had happened. "I'm not sure that we can trust Death, so be very quiet, and I'll think."

I begged not to go to school the next day, but Mama said that I was over my cold and that I would be safer at school in case her trick should fail.

That night when dinner was over, Mama left us reading with Papa and went out. She came back later with a shopping bag full of something that looked like boxes. We asked if she had been shopping, and she said no, she had been to friends borrowing.

Late that night I thought I heard the baby crying, but when I got up to look, he was quietly asleep in his bed.

Mama made me go to school, but I crept back home just before noon. Death was there, in the kitchen. The whole house smelled delicious. Mama had made a big kettle of soup. Death was just finishing a bowl of it.

"I was angry with you yesterday," he said, "but you are a wonderful cook." He held out his bowl for a second helping, then ate it rapidly, spilling some on his robe. "However," he continued between spoonfuls, "you must learn to accept things."

He held out his bowl for another helping. "Who would leave a baby on a bed full of stuffed animals and clean laundry anyway! He might fall off!" He put down his spoon. "I hear the baby crying now. I'll just go get him."

Mama looked stern. "It is rude to ask for thirds and not to finish."

Death finished his soup quickly and headed out the kitchen door. The crying came from the study. Death ran in. No baby, just a tape recorder playing a tape of my little sister crying when she was a baby.

Then we heard another cry. "Wa-a-a-a! Wa-a-a-a!" Death raced up to the baby's bed. Another tape recorder. "Not here!" yelled Death. "Wait. I'll smell him out." But when he sniffed, the whole house was full of the smell of the soup. "Wa-a-a-a," came another long cry from the guest bedroom. But there was another tape recorder. In every room a tape recorder played the calls and cries of babies. Death raced from room to room, his robe flapping. His voice was angrier and angrier. My heart was pounding as I began to count the strokes of the church clock. I could hardly hear it for all of the babies crying . . . six . . . seven . . . eight . . . nine . . . ten . . . eleven . . . . . . twelve.

"You think you're so smart," Death snarled at Mama. "Tomorrow I won't miss."

He slammed the back door. Mama went through the house turning off recorders. Just then the baby awoke and began to call. "Aya, aya, aya." I ran to the pantry. My baby brother was on top of the refrigerator on a bed of clean nappies and towels in his plastic baby bathtub.

As Mama fed the baby, she began to cry. She didn't even scold me for coming home to spy.

"Mama, what will you do now?" I asked as I stroked the baby's fuzzy head. He stopped eating to grin at me. He has no teeth, so it is all gums and drool when he smiles.

"He has only one more try," said Mama.

The next day I had just managed to sneak home and hide when Death arrived. He was early. Mama was holding the baby in her arms when Death walked in the door. On the kitchen table were three loaves of freshly baked bread, a full butter dish and a big bread knife. On the sideboard was a large fat hen Mama was planning to roast for dinner.

Death helped himself to bread and butter. "I'm glad you are going to be reasonable," he said.

"May I just feed him first?" asked Mama softly.

My baby brother gurgled and cooed in her arms. Then he began to chew his fist. "Oh. All right, but no more delay. I can't stand about nattering all day with you. I have work to do," Death complained. He cut another slice of bread and spread the butter on it from edge to edge very carefully before he took a big bite.

Mama wrapped the baby in a big blue flannel blanket and sat down in the kitchen armchair to nurse. Death poured himself a mug of tea and took another slice of bread and butter.

It was nearly twelve when Mama began to burp the baby. The telephone rang. "Answer that, will you please?" Mama said to Death. Death went to the telephone in the front hall.

The baby burped a big one.

Death held the receiver against his chest and leaned around the kitchen door. "It's a carpet-cleaning service. They have a special on this week. Do you want the carpets cleaned?"

"No, thank you," said Mama, as she put the baby to the other breast.

The church clock began to strike twelve. Death slammed down the telephone and ran into the kitchen. "No more fooling!" he said as he snatched the bundle from Mama's arms and rushed out the back door. Mama hid her face in her hands.

The clock was silent. Then we heard Death's angry wail "Cheat! Che-e-e-eat!" he cried. But he didn't come back.

Mama looked up and gave a great big sigh. "He's gone."

Very slowly she leaned over to reach under the table. She

lifted the towel that covered the big bowl we use for making bread. There was my baby brother, chewing on his fist. I couldn't believe my eyes.

"Mama. I didn't see you do that," I said.

Mama pointed to the sideboard, and then picked up my baby brother. I looked to where she pointed and began to laugh and jump up and down. The fat hen was gone.

"Yug-g-g, Mama," I said. "You held that cold thing to your breast!"

Those Three Wishes

No one ever said that Melinda Alice was nice. That wasn't the word used. No, she was clever, even witty. She was called—never to her face, however—Melinda Malice. Melinda Alice was clever and cruel. Her mother, when she thought about it at all, hoped Melinda would grow out of it. To her father, Melinda's very good grades mattered.

It was Melinda Alice, back in the eighth grade, who had labeled the shy, myopic new girl "Contamination" and was the first to pretend that anything or anyone touched by the new girl had to be cleaned, inoculated, or avoided. High school had merely given Melinda Alice greater scope for her talents.

The surprising thing about Melinda Alice was her power; no one trusted her, but no one avoided her either. She was always included, always in the middle. If you had seen her, pretty and witty, in the center of a group of students walking past your house, you'd have thought, "There goes a natural leader."

Melinda Alice had left for school early. She wanted to study alone in a quiet spot she had because there was going to be a big math test, and Melinda Alice was not prepared. That A mattered; so Melinda Alice walked to school alone, planning her studies. She didn't usually notice nature much, so she nearly stepped on a beautiful snail that was making its way across the sidewalk.

"Ugh. Yucky thing," thought Melinda Alice, then stopped. Not wanting to step on the snail accidentally was one thing, but now she lifted her shoe to crush it.

"Please don't," said the snail.

"Why not?" retorted Melinda Alice.

"I'll give you three wishes," replied the snail evenly.

"Agreed," said Melinda Alice. "My first wish is that my next," she paused a split second, "my next thousand wishes come true." She smiled triumphantly and opened her bag to take out a small notebook and pencil to keep track.

Melinda Alice was sure she heard the snail say, "What a clever girl," as it made it to the safety of an ivy bed beside the sidewalk.

During the rest of the walk to school, Melinda was occupied with wonderful ideas. She would have beautiful clothes. "Wish number two, that I will always be perfectly dressed," and she was just that. True, her new outfit was not a lot different from the one she had worn leaving the house, but that only meant Melinda Alice liked her own taste.

After thinking awhile, she wrote, "Wish number three. I wish for pierced ears and small gold earrings." Her father had not allowed Melinda to have pierced ears, but now she had them anyway. She felt her new earrings and shook her beautiful hair in delight. "I can have anything: stereo, tapes, TV videodisc, moped, car, anything! All my life!" She hugged her books to herself in delight.

By the time she reached school, Melinda was almost an altruist; she could wish for peace. Then she wondered, "Is the snail that powerful?" She felt her ears, looked at her perfect blouse, skirt, jacket, shoes. "I could make ugly people beautiful, cure cripples . . ." She stopped. The wave of altruism had washed past. "I could pay people back who deserve it!" Melinda Alice looked at the school, at all the kids. She had an enormous sense of power. "They all have to do what I want now." She walked down the crowded halls to her locker. Melinda Alice could be sweet; she could be witty. She could— The bell rang for assembly. Melinda Alice stashed her books, slammed the locker shut, and just made it to her seat.

"Hey, Melinda Alice," whispered Fred. "You know that big math test next period?"

"Oh, no," grimaced Melinda Alice. Her thoughts raced; "That damned snail made me late, and I forgot to study."

"I'll blow it," she groaned aloud. "I wish I were dead."

A Taste for Quiet

Arthur Tucker was cutting the grass when the stone flew up and struck him squarely on the forehead. Arthur was unconscious for three days. When Arthur came to, he sat straight up in his hospital bed and looked at his wife, who was sitting at the bedside with tears in her eyes.

"May I please have a glass of water?" Arthur asked. Mrs. Tucker handed Arthur a glass full of water. Arthur drank it straight down. "Did someone finish cutting the grass?" asked Arthur, swinging his legs out of bed.

Arthur had been back at home about a week. Life seemed completely normal. He was fairly well caught up at work and on the maintenance of the house, so Arthur stuffed his pipe into his pocket, loaded the canoe and paddle onto his car, and set off for the lake at the edge of town. With some relief, Arthur had learned that no other members of the family felt like canoeing just then.

Arthur had tried, with reasonably good success, to teach each of his children that being companionable did not necessarily demand talk. Now Arthur liked good conversation as well as the next person, but he also loved quiet. And though the children had learned the value of silence individually, when the whole family was together Arthur's ears ached with the constant bickering, with the chitchat, with the talk. True, Arthur adored his children, each and every one. He especially liked to look at and to admire his children while they slept, peacefully, silently.

Arthur paddled out onto the lake to smoke and to enjoy the beautiful tranquil spring day. There was no one in sight. Not a single radio or tape cassette blared. Arthur paddled close to the shore farthest from town. It was filled with violets and spring beauties, from the water's edge clear to the forest.

Quite a bit ahead of him Arthur saw two handsome wild geese with five fluffy yellow goslings swimming between them. Arthur stopped paddling. Slowly, the canoe drifted toward the birds.

"You're crowding me!"

"Swim faster!"

"I can't. She's in the way!"

"Don't push!"

"That's mine!"

"Watch now. There's an old snapping turtle near here."

"Hush, children. Stop your squabbling."

Arthur stared. No one around. But, could he really have understood the geese?

"Good afternoon. Pleasant day for canoeing," nodded the gander to Arthur.

"Yes, it is," Arthur responded before he could even be surprised that he could speak as well as understand.

Arthur pondered a few minutes. That blow on the head must have given him the ability to understand the speech of the geese. He puffed his pipe. Could he understand other birds? He listened. No, just geese.

The gander asked Arthur a few questions. Arthur answered, and out of politeness asked the gander about his life. The gander replied in detail.

These geese no longer migrated from Canada or the north woods to the south and back. They had food enough and a comfortable life all year round right here in town. They had only to avoid the northeast end of the lake because of the hunters who were permitted to shoot from there. It was a different township. The simple truth was, these geese were dull. There was no adventure, no romance, no hardship in their lives. The goslings squabbled; the parents made chitchat about domestic trivia.

As politely as he could, Arthur bade them good day and paddled off.

From then on, the lake was spoiled for Arthur. Any spot free of picnickers with radios and frisbees and chitchat was sure to be full of geese with squabbling goslings and more chitchat.

Summer came and passed through a gray and sodden August to the golden clear days and gentle nights of Indian summer. Those days, too, passed, and the harsh winds of winter came down from Canada.

Arthur Tucker pulled his woollen hat down over his ears and jammed his hands into his pockets. He was nearly home and chilled to his marrow. The wind grew more intense; Arthur rounded the corner next to the church. He had just a block to go. He never heard the crash when the tree split and fell, nor the stone from the church tower when it struck the ground next to him. He never saw the branch that hit him on the head. Arthur was unconscious for four days.

When Arthur came to, he wondered silently to himself if he still understood the speech of geese, but it was weeks before he bothered to check. It really wasn't all that interesting. When he did walk alone down to the lake, he found that his ability to converse with the geese was undiminished, so he went back home. Not until spring did Arthur realize just what the second blow on the head had done.

He was going to bed when he heard a dreadful commotion out in the garden. Some neighbors seemed to be threatening one another in the most abusive language Arthur had ever heard. There was name-calling, then threats of murder and dismemberment, with background discussions of territorial rights. It was all quite unusual in Arthur's fine old neighborhood. Arthur looked out his open window just as one voice snarled, "No! The blue Plymouth is mine!" Arthur looked at the speaker. It was a large, scabrous yellow cat. Once again, Arthur answered before he realized that he could do so.

"I'll thank all of you to stay off the blue Plymouth altogether. Get out!"

Arthur turned back from the window just as the last of Mrs. Tucker's pink curlers retreated beneath the bedcovers.

The dimensions of Arthur's peaceful silence were greatly diminished with the second blow to his head. In order to be disturbed by geese, he had to go to the lake, but cats were everywhere. In retrospect he was amazed that he had failed for so long to notice that he could understand them. Cats talked all the time. Not one of them had anything worth saying. Not one of them could resist waking up from the most comfortable-looking nap in the sun once Arthur appeared. Each cat had to tell Arthur every squalid detail of his or her hunting, fighting, and loving life.

Before summer ended, the cats caused Arthur more trouble. It was a cat shouting, "Look out!" while Arthur was getting into his blue Plymouth that caused him to bump his head, hard, twice: as he went in, and as he came out of the car.

Arthur Tucker has been unconscious for two hours.

Queen Pig

Outside the walls of a great city lived a poor but honest farmer together with his wife and little children. It was late one cold fall evening when the farmer finished his customary walk around his farmyard and stood smoking his pipe beside the pigpen. The first frost had come. Tomorrow he would slaughter the pig. He and his family would taste meat for the first time in many months. There would be sausages, and fat for cooking, and a bit of meat now and then for the long winter ahead.

"Kind farmer," said a low, well-bred voice. The farmer looked around, somewhat surprised. It was the pig who had addressed him so courteously. "Kind farmer," she repeated, "please spare my life, and you shall be well rewarded."

The farmer removed the pipe from his mouth before he replied. "How is it then that you can ask me to spare your life? With my last coin I bought you from my neighbor when you were born, the runt of the litter, too weak to fight for your share of your mother's milk. My neighbor called me foolish, for he had planned to fry you that very night. I have raised you to provide food for me and my family."

"Indeed," replied the pig. "And you and your wife have given me good care. However, I can repay you for your patience, if you will but listen and do as I say: spare me; I shall soon deliver, out of season, twelve fine piglets. Eleven you may sell at the market. The twelfth you must give to the old woman who never grows older. At the proper time, she will come for it. I shall thus give birth every year, each time to twelve, with eleven for you and one for the old woman who never grows older, until my enchantment is ended. So, you see, you shall be repaid, and handsomely, too."

The farmer was silent for a moment before he responded with a question. "There is no evil in what I would do?"

"None," was the pig's firm reply.

"I must speak with my family. They, too, must eat porridge tomorrow and afterward if I spare you."

The pig nodded her agreement, then added, "But none of you must ever speak of our conversation or of any agreement we may make. Such matters are best kept secret."

"Yes, they are," responded the farmer. Bidding her good night, he knocked the ashes from his pipe and went inside.

His wife and older children listened carefully to the farmer's story. When he had finished, they all agreed that they should spare the pig's life and enter into the bargain with her. Each one swore to mention the story to no one. This done, the farmer rose from his chair and strode to the door. Putting on his clogs, he returned to the pig to tell her of their decision so that she would be spared worrying the whole night long.

The pig looked up at him through her long, pale eyelashes and said, "Thank you. You shall not regret your kindness. I shall not speak again until the time of my enchantment has passed."

Again the farmer bade the pig good night and went to bed.

Early the next morning the farmer was going about his daily chores when his neighbor appeared. "What! No fire! For a pig killing you have no fires going by now? Indeed. You did well with that pig with all my good advice on how to care for it." The neighbor sucked his teeth in delicious anticipation before he went on, giving advice freely and commenting on every aspect of the farmer's life, and everyone else's, too, before he repeated his question about the fires.

"No," said the farmer. "I'll not slaughter her today. She seems about to give birth. I'll wait a bit."

This was a bit of news!

"Give birth? Out of season? How can it be? How indeed," repeated the neighbor, "seeing as you have no stud?" At this strange information, he shook his head a good long while.

"I don't quite know myself," replied the farmer. "But I'll soon see."

Scratching his bald pate, the neighbor returned home to his own tidy farm to discuss the matter with his wife. A stingy man, he was regretting more and more the impulsiveness that had led him to sell that weakling piglet.

"Oh," he moaned to his wife, "one just never knows what will happen next with such reckless people as our neighbors, the farmer and his family. Imagine a poor man, with all those children, spending what was probably his last coin for a worthless weakling piglet that was sure to die. And now look. It has become a fine fat pig about to deliver piglets! How can it be?" And he sighed all the day long.

Meanwhile the farmer went quietly about his business.

And so the days passed until the pig did deliver twelve strong piglets. They grew rapidly and well.

One night an old woman appeared at the door. She refused food and drink, nor would she enter the house. "I've come for my piglet," she said grimly.

Unhesitatingly, the farmer went to the pigsty and chose for her the finest of the piglets. Without a word, the old woman stuffed the piglet into her long black sack. The piglet protested briefly, then fell still.

The children stared from behind their mother's skirts in fear. What would the old woman do to the piglet? Was she a witch? She was certainly not anyone they knew.

The next morning the farmer sold the remaining eleven piglets at the market and brought home a purse jingling with coins and a large basket that held two fat hens and a bright loud rooster.

The farmer prospered as the years passed, eleven in a row. Twelve piglets were born each year. Each time the old woman who never grows older came for one of them; the farmer sold the rest. During those years, everything the farmer and his family touched did well. The droppings from the piglets and the chickens made their vegetables and fruit grow wondrously. Their goats and cows produced rich milk, from which they made butter and cheeses. They bought sheep, from whose wool they wove strong, warm clothing.

Because he was a kind man, the farmer shared his wealth

with those less fortunate. Naturally, his neighbor took him to task for squandering his providence. The farmer smiled and went about his business. He paid to have his children taught to read and write. As they grew up, each could learn the trade he or she chose, with a kind master. Though they never mentioned it, the farmer and his family always sold the piglets; they did not eat them, nor did they buy any other piglets to eat during those eleven years. They had a hearty respect for whatever enchantment held the pig and never let their curiosity get the better of them. They did well eating chicken and hoped no hen ever began to talk to them.

Naturally their good fortune did not go unnoticed. Their neighbor spent so much time wondering about all those piglets born out of season, and about the peculiar way the farmer lived, that his own farm suffered a bit for it. How could he have sold such a pig? Surely the crafty farmer had noticed something about it that he had missed. And what was more, the clever farmer was absurdly careful of the old sow who produced such fine piglets. She was not slaughtered, though the years passed. She ate well. She was treated most kindly by the farmer's family. She had her ears scratched by everyone who passed her pen. The neighbor shook his head over the pity of it. He had come to call the old sow "Queen Pig" to himself and to hate her most vehemently. Never had he regretted anything so much as having sold that piglet.

One bitter-cold night the farmer was once again walking around his farmyard, smoking his customary last pipe before going to bed, when once again the pig addressed him most courteously. "Kind farmer, the twelfth year will end tonight. I shall give birth to one last litter of piglets. As soon as I have delivered them I must die."

The farmer felt sorry for the old sow. "We cannot help you?" he asked.

"No," responded the pig, "it is good. My enchantment is over. I shall be released now. But hear me. You must slaughter me after I have delivered, then you must butcher me quickly and do exactly as I say. You must skin me and tan my hide.

My flesh you should use, but burn all of my bones down to the last tiny one; burn them completely to ash, then put the ashes in the garden. Save my hide; it may be of use to you one day."

"Pig," said the farmer, "I don't mean to quibble. But why is it that I should save your hide and burn your bones?"

"It is quite all right to ask," replied the pig patiently. "You know little of magic. Would that I had known less and been less eager to know more. It is enough to say that all of these things are quite specific. The bones must be destroyed quickly because they ultimately cause evil no matter who uses them. The hide can be used only for good, by a good person. The old woman who never grows older cannot use it; I doubt she knows anyone who could. If you need it, you'll know how to use it. Now we should sleep. I shall see you an hour before dawn. Thank you farmer. Good night and good-bye."

The farmer sadly bade the pig good night and turned to go inside. There were many questions he would have liked to ask about the enchantment—who had done it and why—but he doubted she would answer, and he had a healthy respect for whatever magic was operating. Instead he turned back and said, "Pig, thank you for all you have done for us. I am sorry for what you have endured."

"Thank you. You have all been kinder to me than I could have expected," replied the pig.

With that, the farmer went inside to tell his family that tomorrow they must invite all the neighbors to the traditional feast that accompanies a pig killing.

As was his custom, the farmer's neighbor came around the next morning quite early. He was astonished to see that the pig had been slaughtered and butchered and that sausages had already been made.

"Good morning," said the farmer's eldest daughter. "My father was just going to send the little ones to tell all the neighbors that we shall have a pig killing feast today. Perhaps you'll carry the message on your morning round of visits?"

In the courtyard a fire burned brightly, crackling and

spitting. Over the flames hung a great black pot in which the pig's lard bubbled and steamed.

"Ho! Ho!" shouted the neighbor. "The early bird catches the worm. You are nearly done with a day's work." Then he saw the farmer and his wife squeezing milk from leather bags into the mouths of the twelve hungry piglets.

"What? Slaughtered the pig with a new litter? What will you think of next?"

"The birth was too much for her. She was dying," replied the farmer.

"Ah," said the neighbor. "So Queen Pig is dead. Do you want to sell a piglet?"

"Perhaps," replied the farmer. "Will you and your family come to the feast?"

"Yes, of course," was the eager reply.

The neighbor heard an odd sound. Though he turned to listen more carefully, he could not make it out.

The feeding finished, the farmer's wife went inside the house. The farmer stirred the fire, then left his youngest child to watch it. Bidding his neighbor good day, he went into the barn to tend to the cow. The neighbor stood by the fire listening. Among the pieces of flaming wood sputtered and crackled a fine, juicy bone. As it sizzled it seemed to hiss, "Eat me! Eat me!"

"Waste not, want not," said the neighbor as he set to work with a stick to poke the bone out of the fire.

"No, no," said the child. "We must burn the bone."

"Children should be seen and not heard," said the neighbor, carefully putting the still hot and smoking bone into his sack. "If you are so rich that you can waste good bones, others are not. We'll use this for our dinner tomorrow." Off he marched. All the way home he told himself that finally he was in some small measure compensated for the piglet he had so foolishly sold to the farmer all those years ago.

The child ran sobbing to tell her father. By the time the farmer returned to the courtyard, the neighbor was out of sight.

The neighbor, with his sack, arrived home to find his wife just setting breakfast upon the table. Triumphantly he pulled out the bone. "Look, wife. A fine bone for tomorrow's dinner. Queen Pig finally died and today we are invited to the farmer's for the feast. Imagine, he was burning this juicy bone."

"Perhaps the beast was diseased," worried his wife.

"No, no. The man is just a fool, too rich to care, I'll wager," replied her husband, settling down to eat. He put the bone in front of him on the table.

"Careful," said his wife. "I've just washed the floor. Don't drip grease from that bone all over the place."

Just then their son came in for his breakfast. "What's this?" he asked, picking up the bone.

"It is a bone the farmer wanted to burn, the wasteful fellow! But you will be glad to hear that he has invited us to his pig killing feast this day," replied the neighbor.

"Oh," said the son. "Indeed I am glad. I do want to go, if not for the fine food, then just to see the farmer's beautiful eldest daughter." He sighed. "I wish my load of wood were all cut and in the cart so that I would surely be ready in time."

Hardly were the words out of his mouth when they heard the cheerful clatter of logs tumbling into the bin beside the hearth. Once it was full, the sound continued as the cart standing in the courtyard filled, too.

"Thunder and lightning!" shouted the neighbor, grabbing the bone from his astonished son. "So that is what the farmer has been up to with Queen Pig. Ah! I wish I had all those bones of hers from the fire."

His words still hung in the air when a pile of charred bones and greasy ashes appeared upon the table. As the neighbor and his family watched, the smoking mess slid from the table to the benches and the floor.

Furious, the neighbor's wife took the bone from her husband's hand. "Oh! I wish you could not say such foolish things! Look at this mess!"

The neighbor wanted to reply, but his mouth was sealed

shut. His wife ignored the fury in his eyes while she got to work with broom and rags and a pail of soapy water. Soon the bones were all in a pot, and the kitchen was clean once more. The neighbor looked at his wife. Fearful pleading had replaced the anger in his eyes.

Taking the bone in her wet and soapy hands, the neighbor's wife said, "I wish my husband had his power of speech once again."

"Now, my dear," said the neighbor in a great rush. "We must see if all the bones are powerful. Imagine that scoundrel with a magic pig all these years. Why, he could have been king."

Shaking his head at his parents' folly, the neighbor's son finished his meal and departed to deliver his wood. "Don't wish anything for me. The load of wood is enough. I will see you at the feast."

The neighbor and his wife were too engrossed with the bone to do more than nod at their son. They soon set to work to test the other bones with diverse small, careful wishes.

Meanwhile the farmer comforted his youngest child as best he could. He told her that probably no harm would come if the neighbor ate just one of the pig's bones. He did not believe the words himself, but hoped they might prove true. The day's work left him little time for worry. There was much to do before the guests arrived for the feast. Not only had they a normal day's farm work and the preparations for the feast to do, but twelve lusty piglets to feed until their little bellies bulged with warm milk and they snuffled happily in their sleep. He and his wife and children worked hard all day, with barely a moment to discuss the missing bone.

The day passed quickly. The guests began to arrive. Inside the house the whole ground floor room was filled from end to end with one long table. On it there were steaming soup with liver dumplings; platters of sauerkraut with pork; thick slices of bread; potatoes and parsley; blood sausage, liver sausage, and spicy pork-meat sausage; all to be washed down with young red wine. For dessert there were bowls of tart apples, nuts, and baked sweets of tender pastry filled with fruits and nuts.

After dinner the children stretched out upon the floor awhile to rest their stomachs. Soon revived, they began to play under, beside, and around the table. The grown-ups settled down to talk.

There was never any lack of matter for conversation, but even less so at this pig killing feast. The neighbor and his wife had arrived last, dressed in a most unusual fashion. She was decked out in an astonishing array of laces and ribbons, and he tottered in wearing high-heeled shoes such as he had once seen on market day in the great city. No one, not even the farmer, understood their words of greeting: "Well, well. Now we, too, finally share in the wonderful good fortune of the pig." The other guests whispered and shook their heads, assuming the neighbor referred to the food at the feast. But what an odd thing to say to the farmer, who was always so generous.

What's more, the neighbor's wife was quick to take offence today. Several times she said in a most threatening manner that one must not slight her or that one would be sure to regret it.

What with the peculiar behavior of the neighbor and his wife, and the usual talk of crops and weather, of taxes and war, of animals and children, it was a lively evening.

But there were some who did not wish to take part in the noisy, cheerful scene. The first was the farmer's youngest child. She continued to reproach herself for allowing the neighbor to take the bone and for thus disobeying the pig's solemn warning that the bones, all the bones, must be burned. Unable to eat or drink, she finally pulled on a cloak and went quietly outside.

It was nearly dark, and very cold. By the time the child reached the neighbor's door she was shivering though she clutched the cloak around her. There she stood. She could hardly breathe for fear. She was about to break one of the basic laws of their life: one must never enter another's house without being asked. Trembling violently, she reached for the latch, then stopped. From inside came the sounds of many tiny voices. Fairies? Evil spirits? Robbers? Gradually, determination and curiosity overcame her fear, and she cautiously opened the door.

The only light in the room came from the embers on the fireplace grate. The voices seemed to come from a pot near the fireplace. Slowly, as quietly as possible, the child crept over to the pot.

Inside the pot, many somewhat charred, ill-mannered bones were jostling one another and pleading, "Take me! Take me! Take me!"

"Magic piggy bones. Take. Take. Take."

"Put me in your dolly. I'll tell you stories and sing to you in the night."

"No, take *me*. When your little legs are tired, I'll carry you to school faster than the wind."

"No-o-o-o, me. I'll make you a princess."

"Me. I'll get you all the sweets you could desire."

"Me. Me, me, me. Wish, wish, wish."

The child closed her eyes to make a wish. But wait! She'd come to burn the pig's bone. Aloud she said, "No, I don't want you!" She picked up the pot and looked closely at the bones. The one she had come for was much bigger than those. No, it certainly was not in the pot. Had the neighbor hidden it or eaten it?

"Oh, now what will I do?" she cried. "I just wish I had the bone I came for." Thunk! It fell into the pot with the others.

"Thank God!" cried the child gratefully and ran to the fireplace.

"No. No, no!" screeched the bones as she threw them all onto the embers.

Up flared the fire. The bones were soon gone.

Carefully she put the pot back in its place, went out, and closed the door.

Home she ran, stumbling often in the darkness.

Two others were also reluctant to take part in the general

conversation and storytelling after dinner. The farmer's eldest daughter went out to feed the piglets. The neighbor's son went to help her. His parents, the perpetual busybodies, had, through some fortunate accident, produced a son totally unlike themselves. He was a kind, cheerful, and, truth to say, good-looking young man, who worked hard, liked to laugh, and loved the farmer's eldest daughter.

These two sat quietly in the barn feeding the twelve piglets one by one from leather sacks filled with warm cow's milk. After a while the girl ventured, "Your parents are not quite themselves tonight."

"No," replied the young man a bit absently, for he was not thinking of his parents just then. "Must be the magic bones and all the wishes."

The startled girl neglected her piglet for a second or two; the poor little thing began to choke. Stopping to burp him, she looked at the neighbor's son.

"Magic bone?" she repeated.

"Yes, I was holding a bone when they told me about the feast today at your house. I said that I wished I'd be done with my work so that I could come. The work was done before I had finished speaking. My parents then set to wishing with a will." He laughed indulgently.

"I see," said the girl, putting down the sleeping piglet and taking up another.

Clearly, the subject of the magic bone was of little interest to the young man, and he passed on to other matters that were closer to both their hearts.

Once the piglets were fed, the two returned to the house. The farmer's youngest child had come inside and climbed into her mother's lap. She was fast asleep.

When the last guest had gone, the farmer's eldest daughter told the rest of the family about the magic in the bones. Some of her brothers wanted to go to the neighbor and demand that the bones be burned before something dreadful happened. Their father merely smoked his pipe and shook his head. Finally he said, "He'd never do it."

"He can't. I already did it," said a tearful, sleepy voice from their mother's lap. The youngest child fearfully told them where she had been and what she had done.

"Perhaps this is the end of it," said the farmer's wife. "A few ribbons and some silly shoes. But I, for one, will be glad when the twelfth piglet is taken away by the old woman who never grows older." At the mention of the old woman who never grows older, they all shivered. Somehow no one believed that the mischief was truly over.

Certainly their neighbor gave them no peace. He was over before dawn the next morning, all hot and disheveled. He and his wife had been up all night trying to find the bones, trying to call them back with whatever approximations of magic they could muster. They had failed. "You have used magic to deny me magic. I'll have you before the king!" he threatened. Nothing they did would calm him. He departed, still muttering threats.

A week passed. Then another. The neighbor rarely appeared. The weather turned colder; night came earlier. No one went about much. The farmer finished tanning the pig's hide. His wife folded it and put it into a trunk in the bedroom. "I do wonder what power it possesses," said the farmer's eldest daughter when she closed the lid of the trunk.

"The pig said that when the time came to use it we would know," responded the farmer without much conviction.

Another week passed. Soon the snows would come, perhaps even tonight. It was nearly bedtime when they heard a knock at the door. It was the old woman who never grows older.

"I've come for my pig."

"Isn't it still too small?" protested the farmer.

"Not for me."

Someone fetched a piglet. The old woman stuffed it into a bag that was already nearly full of something that wriggled violently. The wind blew in at the open door. The old woman who never grows older stepped forward on the doorstep.

"And I'll take that one, too," she said, reaching for the farmer's youngest child.

"What?" said the farmer. "She is not yours."

"Indeed she is. She wished upon the wretched queen's bones. She is owed to me now!" With that, the old woman who never grows older pointed a fat yellow finger at the child, who immediately grew smaller and smaller until she was the size of a little doll. The old woman who never grows older popped her into the bag and turned to go.

The farmer's eldest daughter knew what she must do. She sprang to the chest, threw it open, and grabbed the pigskin. Swiftly she ran after the old woman who never grows older, who dropped her bag and turned to point her fat yellow finger at the approaching girl. But it was too late. The pigskin was already thrown over her. When they lifted the skin, she was smaller than an ant and still shrinking. Out of the bag tumbled two rats, the piglet, and two tiny dolls; one was the farmer's youngest child, the other the neighbor's son. Squeaking and chattering, the two rats dashed off to the barn. The girl quickly threw the skin over the dolls and the piglet. There stood the neighbor's son, her little sister, and a handsome boy dressed in fine clothes of a foreign fashion.

Everyone began to talk at once. The boy thanked them and begged the use of the skin in order to end the enchantment of his eleven brothers and sisters. The others fell silent to hear his story. Queen Pig was their mother. She had indeed been a queen. The queen, having made herself accomplished in magic, had run afoul of the old woman who never grows older, who was a powerful witch. The old woman who never grows older had cursed the hapless queen with the dreadful punishment of being reborn as a pig and living to see each of her twelve children born as piglets, to be taken away by the witch to serve her until someone, or something, perhaps only death, would end the enchantment.

The boy planned to journey to the dwelling of the old woman, who was no more, and free his brothers and sisters and any others he might find there.

"We shall also need the skin to free my parents, if we can find them," added the neighbor's son.

"Your parents?" repeated the others.

"Yes . . . the two rats that ran to the barn. She changed them into rats when they argued with her in our kitchen."

It was agreed to cut off enough of the skin to cover a rat, and to send the larger portion with the young prince.

Time passed. In the spring the neighbor's son and the farmer's daughter were wed. Among the gifts that arrived for the wedding were twelve beautiful plates of a foreign design and a piece of pig's hide.

The farmer's eldest daughter sewed it to the piece they had saved and placed it in a trunk in the bedroom. Though they put it over each and every rat they caught, they never found the neighbor and his wife. After each attempt, the skin was returned to the trunk, and, if it has not been lost, it remains there still.

Odd Jobs

Miss Hetty cleared her throat and began to speak. "Our brother, who, unfortunately, is away on a trip . . ."

Miss Letty giggled. Miss Netty gave her a hard look, and Miss Hetty continued.

"Perhaps I should add that you were not the first teen-agers we hired through the Youth Employment Service, but we had despaired of finding anyone who could assist us.

"You see, we need something more than just the help one would expect to provide three old ladies living in a large old house. There are those tasks, of course, and you have done splendidly. But you two have qualities about you that make me think that you can provide the assistance we truly need, which is something more.

"Our brother left us a series of puzzles, little tasks to be done. It was, well, a prank, a series of jokes on us. I'm afraid he was a bit annoyed with us for some little jokes we played on him. I should add that when these pranks began, we were all quite a bit younger than we are now." She looked at John and Jane, then continued.

"One reason we needed the cleaning you have done was so that we could look carefully for any clues or messages he might have left us in any of those storage areas you so beautifully tidied up for us."

John nearly groaned aloud at the thought. Every time he and Jane had got something straightened out, one of the three elderly sisters would begin to rummage through the stuff just one more time.

"Surely," continued Miss Hetty, "you can help us now?"

John looked at Jane, then shrugged his assent.

Jane was having a terrible time concentrating on what Miss Hetty was saying. That music, wild and sad—someone must be playing some sort of flute or reed. It was always here in the old ladies' house, but now it was so loud that Jane could barely sit still. How could the others not hear it? She wondered if she was cracking up. Jane looked around her. Miss Hetty was waiting for an answer.

"Oh yes, yes. I think we can help. At least we can try," Jane finally stammered.

She must ask John about the music. It seemed the minute she left the place she always forgot, except that lately she had begun to hear it in her head at odd times during the day and night. Beautiful tune, so sad.

Miss Hetty continued. "One task is to decipher a verse and then to do what it says. It was given in Greek, not that it matters particularly, and then in wretched German doggerel."

"And the English is nearly as bad," interjected Miss Letty.

"True," replied Miss Hetty. "Here it is."

> Wait for the silver, and you'll miss the gold;
> Fail this year and the increase is hundred-fold.

For a minute, everyone looked at everyone else in silence. Finally, Jane asked, although she was never sure why, "Would you mind saying it in Greek? It won't help us to understand, but I'd just like to hear it."

Miss Hetty read, and Jane's future was set.

Of the twins, John was the one who was all eyes for seeing the world and hands for drawing it. His notebook margins and every scrap of paper he touched were filled with drawings. At athletics, he had driven the coach to distraction his first season with that sketch pad. Except for when he was warming up or actually in an event, John drew all the time. Coach had opposed the sketching as "too much use of small muscles, with too much concentration." But when John set records and won races, Coach relaxed.

Jane clearly had an ear for music, for languages, for

people's accents, and for their stories. She wasn't sure how she would put her talents to work, for she played the piano as much for escape as for pleasure in making music, and she often felt she read without much discrimination simply because the books were there. Now the language of that puzzle captured her completely.

The twins left the house, promising the old ladies that they would come back as soon as they had some ideas about the puzzle. No, it wouldn't be tomorrow. They had to do some work at home. April was hot this year and everything in the garden was rushing into bloom.

For a few blocks they walked without talking.

"Money in the bank increases from year to year," muttered Jane, "but so would golden daffodils or tulips in the garden." She gestured toward the flowers along the way, petals now closed for the night.

John nodded. He wondered whether Jane had thought of money for the same reason he had. They were nearly home. He had already begun to hope that Aunt Nasturtium's car would not be in the driveway. Lately she had had a most unsettling habit of arriving to check on them whenever the old ladies had not paid the twins for more than a few days. The old ladies needed them nearly every day after school, but they paid them at odd intervals.

Aunt Nasturtium was their father's sister. She saw it as her mission in life to drive Daddy to "success." Every visit brought a lecture on how their father surely would get his reward in Heaven, since he certainly wasn't getting it on earth. Each birthday, every Christmas, produced a book that declared that success demanded this or that generally unscrupulous practice, outlined what to do and how to do it, and had quizzes at the end of every chapter. Daddy said, "Thank you," and never opened a single one. Lately Aunt Nasturtium seemed to be turning her attention toward Jane and John.

"Whew," John sighed.

"She's not there," observed Jane with obvious relief. "It doesn't explain the silver," she said, returning to the puzzle, "but then money can be silver, too."

"I don't know," John shrugged. "I'm too hungry to think. Who is cook tonight? Dad?"

In a town where everyone was named Candace, Kimberly, Hardy, or Meredith, it was hard to be named Jane and John, and to be twins at that. It was as if their parents had been too surprised at getting two of them to do much about calling them something a bit less, well, ordinary. John had once wondered aloud whether having a sister named Nasturtium had perhaps prejudiced their father, at least against anything but the very simplest of names.

Then when they were in the eighth grade, Mother had died. Daddy, bless him, had successfully resisted Aunt Nasturtium's offer to move in with them. Her frequent visits, however, were to be endured.

The next morning Jane and John set to work on the things they had neglected at home while they had been working for the three old ladies on Hawthorne Terrace. They cleaned the garage and the shed, then cut and trimmed the grass.

Jane found herself repeating the puzzle verse while she dug. "Wait for the silver, and you'll miss the gold." With a certain satisfaction, she set to work on the dandelions. They used their mother's old tactic: "Every day take out the ones that have flowered. Then you'll clear the lawn. Do it every year and the dandelions never take over, though some will always blow onto the lawn from somewhere else and reseed themselves." This system of taking them out was much less discouraging than to be assigned the job: dig out *all* the dandelions!

Although Jane followed her mother's dictum, she sometimes also took out a green dandelion plant near one in flower. Getting ahead of them that way made her feel she'd tricked them and gave her a small triumph.

Jane dug viciously at a plantain. These were tougher birds than the dandelions. The dandelion root was long and slim, easy to pry out, but the plantain root went tenaciously in every direction.

"Never saw a flower on these wretched things. Can't eat them. Wonder what use they are," she gritted through her teeth as she attacked another one.

"John! I think I've got it!" she yelped. Then, feeling silly, she looked around to see if anyone else had heard her.

"What?" he brushed the sweat from his forehead.

"Dandelions are gold . . ."

"Sure! Then silver, and if you don't dig them out, it sure is a hundred-, maybe a thousand-fold." Then he groaned. "Have you noticed the lawn at the old ladies' house? It will take us weeks to clear it."

"Goody," Jane responded without much enthusiasm. She sighed. "At least it's out of doors, better than cleaning closets and attics."

"Yeah," John replied. "But why did their brother make a puzzle out of it? Why not just leave them a note to weed the lawn?"

"Funny about dandelions," John said later. "Once, up in the Adirondacks, I came out of the cabin, must have been May, early spring up there. The ground was still kinda bare, so I really noticed a pretty yellow flower in the clearing. I thought, gee, that's nice, too early for Indian paintbrush though, and never saw a yellow one. When I went over to see, it was a dandelion, very thin, with just one flower, three long leaves, not a single green bud showing below on the ground. All alone there on the brown grass it was beautiful. I always liked them after that." He paused. "Until tomorrow, when we start the old ladies' lawn."

The next day when the twins reported their solution to the puzzle, the three ladies were strangely unresponsive. Finally Miss Hetty recovered herself and smiled at them.

"Thank you. It will be a miserable job for you, and I am sorry. We had hoped that the solution to the puzzle would be somewhat . . . somewhat more helpful to us." She turned away. "Thank you. Please let me know how long it takes you to do it so we can pay you accordingly."

It took several days. By the time the twins were finished

with the job, the rains came. April had been the last month of a long drought. Now May brought four weeks of rain. And when the rains came, the old ladies disappeared. Jane and John reported for work to find only notes for them in a silent, empty house.

Silent for the most part, that is; silent except for the music, which Jane heard less often now. It was always faint, sometimes so faint that she strained to hear it.

Gone, too, was the characteristic smell of the house, the one Jane had tried unsuccessfully to identify. It was pleasant, fresh, but not like air fresheners—they made Jane sneeze. No, this was a smell she should know; one she did know, but couldn't name. It hadn't seemed to belong there. Now it was gone.

The twins went to the old ladies' house as often as they could. In the house they found notes, but not the old ladies. The notes rarely requested work, and never included any payment; they did, however, give permission to use the library in the house. Working there was useful. Jane and John got a great deal of studying done and they could avoid a good number of Aunt Nasturtium's visits.

She never let up. How would they pay for college? How could they continue to work for three old ladies who paid them so erratically? Where *were* the old ladies? Aunt Nasturtium threatened to go to the head of the Youth Employment Service.

Then she was off on a new tack. The twins should be with young people more. They should study more—or less, depending on her mood. Daddy was used to her; he could take it without getting mad. The twins had not yet developed that talent.

The old-fashioned library was a pleasant refuge. Its shelves went from floor to ceiling and were crammed with books, except for a single shelf of large conch shells. The long library table in the center of the room had three good reading lamps, piles of books, and an enormous glass jar with a heavy glass stopper, the kind you'd find in a grocer's a hundred years ago. The jar was full of small seashells. John had already drawn it, and some of the large shells, and the room, and the few old fragments of vases and amphorae, and the old ladies as well.

He drew Jane while she read. His sketch pads filled rapidly. Those pads were just one more reason they needed to be paid for their work. They tried never to hit Dad for money. After their mother's long illness, he had plenty to pay for as it was.

So when the old ladies neglected to pay them, it *was* inconvenient, but John and Jane had grown fond of them. Besides, it was awful to have Aunt Nasty always be right. Instead of facing her, the twins escaped to the cool old house to read and draw.

"I wonder if Miss Hetty used to be a professor of, say, Greek literature," mused Jane one evening. "So many books in Greek, and on Greek literature, on Greece. It's like being turned loose on a feast."

"Then Miss Netty, with her husky voice and her purple dresses, was probably an art history professor, I'd say," added John, hoisting a large tome. "I've never seen such beautiful stuff."

"And Miss Letty?" Jane looked up. "Poor thing. Everything she touches spills and drops. She always complains about 'this' body. Sometimes, when she is still, though, she's as beautiful, as graceful as a dancer in repose, or like one of these." She touched a fragment of a vase on which was painted the silhouette of an acrobat. "Maybe she was a dancer and was sick or injured."

"Funny," added John, "she did say once when she spilled something how she had not always been like this. But that is the only reference any of them has ever made to the past, their past. They are full of stories about—" John stopped. "What's the matter?"

Jane had started out of her chair.

"What?" insisted John.

"It's stopped," whispered Jane.

"What's stopped?"

"The music. It broke off without finishing. It often grows faint, but it always finishes. Lately it has been faint. Sometimes it used to be really loud."

"*What* music?" asked John, looking around the room.

"Oh. It drives me wild. I keep meaning to ask you or the ladies whether you hear it, but I always seem to forget or something interrupts me. Then I hear it here," she tapped her forehead. "It's a sad, lonely song, played on some sort of flute. It has lots of variations, but always the same theme. Sometimes it's very loud, but lately it's been so faint, I find myself straining to hear it. Now it stopped in the middle, just like that."

"Music, empty house, nutty old ladies . . . Let's go home. I'm starved. Never did see any food here," said John, gathering up his pad, books, and pencils.

"Me neither. Where can the old ladies be? All the time we've known them they have never once gone out shopping, to doctors, dentists, on visits, nothing you'd expect three old ladies to do. So why should they leave when it rains? When they come back I will ask them about the music, first thing."

She slammed her books together. John locked the door behind them. Jane was hungry, too. She forgot to ask John about the smell.

In June, the sun reappeared with sudden intensity. The world became dry, limp with heat. On the first day of sunshine, Jane went directly to Hawthorne Terrace after school. The minute she let herself in the front door, she knew that the ladies were back in the house. Jane stopped in the hall. The smell had returned. It was overpowering and confusing because it shouldn't have been there. Then suddenly she knew: it smelled like the ocean. She almost expected the wind to blow. But why? And how? The ocean was several hours away by car.

The music started up again. Jane listened to it, feeling such overwhelming sadness that she thought she would weep. She listened so intently that a few minutes passed before she realized she was eavesdropping on a quarrel.

Miss Netty and Miss Letty were both talking at once, both very angry. Then Miss Hetty was lecturing her sisters in firm, measured sentences.

"It is no use finding fault with one another. Our brother tricked us into assuming human shape, here so far from the sea, and now we must complete the tasks so that he will release us. We are nearly done. Please do not quarrel. These mortal twins are helping us." She sighed. "I do admit that I am disturbed, too. Where is our brother hiding to watch us suffer here? Has this not gone on too long? We are aging in these human shapes."

At that Miss Letty began to sob. "Like poor Tithonus, we'll become dried-up little crickets."

Miss Hetty's voice grew gentler. "Ah, don't cry, dear. The rains did make it possible for us to return to the sea for a short time. That was a gift. Now, don't cry. I know that we are nearly done."

Jane slipped out as quietly as she could. The music wailed behind her.

John had started home but had seen Aunt Nasturtium's car and turned back, trying to decide whether to go to school, to the public library, or to Hawthorne Terrace. With a shrug for Aunt Nasturtium, he headed for the house on Hawthorne Terrace. He would ask the old ladies about that music Jane kept hearing. Instead, he found Miss Letty standing in the living room weeping. The floor and the furniture were covered with a thick layer of straight pins.

"Box explode?" asked John sympathetically.

"May as well have," whimpered Miss Letty. "Why, why, why is my brother so mean? I'll never get all of them picked up. They keep spilling again and again. Day after day it is the same."

John tried not to stare. For a minute she looked like a little child standing there.

"I'll get something to pick them up," he reassured her. "Wait here; I'll be right back."

54

He rushed out the door and ran home. With a brief "Hi, sorry, gotta rush" to Aunt Nasturtium, he was in and out of his room and back at Hawthorne Terrace.

Miss Hetty came in just as he swept the large bar magnet once more over the floor. This time there was not a single pin on the bar. John looked carefully. The floor was clean. Cautiously, holding her breath, Miss Letty handed Miss Hetty the full, closed box.

"Done!" cried Miss Hetty. "That was one I feared you'd never do." She turned to John. "Thank you. We are nearly done with our tasks. There is just one more."

"One impossible one," said Miss Netty as she came into the room. "It is something for Heracles."

"The task," continued Miss Hetty, "is to draw a team of four horses and a cart from New York to Philadelphia in one passage of the sun through the skies."

"Meaning sunup to sundown?" asked John.

"I suppose so," replied Miss Hetty, "but—"

John chuckled. "I can do it tomorrow, Saturday, easily."

The ladies looked bewildered. John left without explaining.

It was late that night before Jane had a chance to tell John what she had overheard. "Even knowing more about who they are, or what they are, doesn't help us to help them. They sounded so miserable. Even if the music didn't tear me up, I'd still feel sorry for them."

"Well," John yawned. "Let's see if I can do the last job for them tomorrow. And you can ask about the music."

Jane nodded. "Then we can tell them what we know. We'll see."

John returned late the next day, triumphantly bearing a large sketch pad. "Four people offered to buy it," he grinned.

Miss Hetty, Miss Letty, and Miss Netty crowded around. Jane watched.

"See? I drew a four-horse team pulling a chariot, which seemed more attractive than a mere farm cart. I drew it all the way from New York to Philadelphia, on the train. Does that do?"

Proper Miss Hetty whooped for joy. "Now we must be done! We did most of our brother's silly tasks and you two, thank you, have done the rest. I thought he would be here to watch our struggle. For some reason he has hidden from us. Now he can come back. Where is he?" she demanded in a voice that rang through the silent house. "He *must* come and set us free!"

The three ladies looked around. No one came. In the silence that followed, Miss Letty began to cry without a sound. Jane heard the music start up again, faint, slow, so incredibly sad. All three ladies looked broken, weary, old.

"That music," Jane whispered. "Can't anyone hear it?"

"Music?" repeated Miss Netty.

"It sounds like this but it's played on a flute or pipes of some sort." Jane opened the piano and began to play along with the music she had heard so many times.

All three sisters stared at Jane in horror.

"Is this another trick?" whispered Miss Hetty.

"Oh, no!" interrupted Miss Letty. "I remember now! I hid our brother's pipes. Then when I learned that he had tricked us and trapped us, I was so upset that I forgot."

She ran to the jar of seashells and removed the stopper. It took both hands to lift the jar. Miss Letty poured the shells out onto the table. "I must have surprised him in his own flute," she murmured. In the middle of the soft pastels of the seashells lay double panpipes of wood or reed.

Jane wasn't sure what she saw next—a flash of curved leg, of hoof, then a man in elegant, rather old-fashioned clothes standing in the doorway as if he had been there watching them for quite a few minutes. He was pale and a bit worn, but handsome.

"We have had enough of jokes, haven't we?" he asked.

All three sisters rushed to him.

"Indeed we have," sighed Miss Hetty. "Now we can go home."

"You must be patient a bit longer and wait for rain," he replied.

Miss Letty groaned. Her face still glistened with tears.

Her brother gently patted her hand.

"You have my promise. You will soon be home. Someone clearly has taken pity on us all or else you would not have had the help of these twins, and this little adventure, which has gone on for too long, might never have ended." He bowed most formally to Jane and John. "Thank you. Before we leave, we must give you your payment." Miss Hetty went to her desk and took out a rather large leather purse.

"Here it is," she said, pulling out one bill after another. "Here is payment for all those hours for which you have not yet been paid. That, too, was part of our task, to find someone willing to help us even when we did not pay as regularly as we ought. We had been silly and selfish for so long with our constant tricks and jokes, and our jealousy of our brother's freedom to come and go as he wished, on sea or land, that he decided to teach us a lesson."

"But our brother, too, was caught," added Miss Letty.

"If I am not being too inquisitive," said Jane, tentatively, "if you are, as I suppose, Nereids, I thought you were sisters. I never read about a brother."

"We are fifty sisters, in fact," replied Miss Hetty. "Our brother is never mentioned in the stories. He is, perhaps, not a brother exactly. We are not to ask, but he was raised as a brother and is half of the sea and half of the land."

"A brother is what I am," chuckled the pale gentleman, "and the only thing I want is my pipes." Striding to the table, he quickly took them up and pocketed them.

A week later Aunt Nasturtium brought a tuna casserole for dinner. When they had finished eating, she repeated the story as the twins had told it to her, which was with numerous omissions. She repeated it triumphantly as a lesson well learned.

"The brother returned abruptly and asked you to bring a lawyer and witnesses to the house. He said the sisters could not leave unless you did this. So you did. He paid the lawyer to make out a deed giving the house and all its contents to you two. After the lawyer left, there was a great thunderstorm. The ladies kissed you good-bye and left, in the rain. And the brother? He left, too." She chuckled complacently. "Well, well, wages *and* a house full of books and antiques. So that's why you stuck it out, and were so sweet to those old ladies. You two *are* clever, far cleverer than I thought. Well done!"

Jane shuddered. Aunt Nasturtium's praise was worse than her blame. Daddy looked pained. John sat stonily silent, sketching away. Jane glanced at him. John tilted the pad slightly so that she could see. The page was dense with fauns, satyrs and centaurs, all playing pipes. From ocean waves and foam rose shells and Nereids with the faces of young girls, and with the faces of old women; one face was weeping.

"Can you play that song again?" he whispered.

Low Hurdles

Jeff hadn't listened to me all day. I gave up and simply watched, waiting for the disaster, hoping it would not come.

The fire was perfect. It had burned down until the two big logs glowed, with flames licking the air between them. Jeff looked around the room with pleasure. Two loaves of bread, one French, one sour black Russian rye; some salami, cheeses, and butter; red wine and a bowl of fruit; it was all there on the low table between two comfortable chairs. There was enough light to read by. Jeff nodded to himself. Yes, it was all ready. He knew just what they'd talk about. First there'd be sports, skiing, hockey, and winter in general; then he'd ask Brian about the seminar he'd come down to teach, and about wrestling, then about Brian's new book.

Brian would ask him about sport, school, and then he'd ask, "Well, what are you writing?" or, "Write anything lately?" Something like that. Jeff knew he'd shrug, then bring out the folder. He had the stories all ready. He'd debated where to put the one he'd done first, the one the publisher had seen and liked, the one that got the collection going. Should it be on the top? On the bottom? Jeff compromised. He put it in the middle.

By now it wasn't even the best he'd done, but "Low Hurdles" was the first one that had shown he was a writer. He wouldn't tell Brian that the collection was sold, that it would be a book. Not yet. He wanted to give his cousin a printed copy. Not that Brian would be jealous. No, he wasn't that way. Brian had worked hard for his own success, and he had been young, too, when he made it. Not that Jeff felt he'd made it, not by a long shot. But . . . No, Jeff wanted to keep his secret to himself for a while. He wanted not just the promise of his book, but the book itself.

Jeff hadn't heard the car drive up, so the sharp clack of the front-door knocker startled him. In two strides he was at the door.

Brian looked up at him and grinned. "Hey, kid! When will you stop growing? Good thing you don't want to wrestle; you'd be too long for the mats." He turned back and gestured toward the snow that lay knee-deep outside. "This is beautiful! Nice greeting for a New Englander."

"Yeah," Jeff agreed. "I love it. But enjoy it now because by the time you get your skis up from the basement to head for some local approximation of a hill, it could be a toasty sixty degrees outside."

"I remember. Fastest weather in the world. Oversleep and you miss spring."

"Spring?" replied Jeff. "Oh, yes. I remember. Last year it was on a Friday, between three and four in the afternoon. Beautiful."

While they completed the Old Family Weather Routine, they went inside. Then, for a while, everything did go as Jeff had imagined. Brian was hungry after the long drive. Jeff was always hungry. They ate well, talking of this and that. The words and hours flew. Finally, Brian did ask the question, and Jeff handed his cousin the folder of stories and busied himself with the fire, waiting. Brian held the folder for a moment without opening it.

"Jeff," he began, "I want to tell you something I've been thinking about recently. You know, I remember when you were born. But I especially remember when you were about two, my little buddy. It was great to grow up with a little guy around, one who always thought you were great, even when the rest of the world didn't. When everything was lousy, there was that faithful little hero-worshiper. Not many people have that. I just wanted to tell you. You're okay, always have been, even though the little guy got to be such a bean pole."

Ducking the wad of paper Jeff threw at him, Brian opened

the folder and started to read. He laughed in all the right places. He seemed pleased. Jeff heard an occasional low "Nice, very nice." By the time Brian had finished the third story, he looked up.

"I'd like to show these to someone."

Now that response hadn't occurred to Jeff. He merely shrugged and poked the fire again. I was getting nervous. Finally there was nothing more to be done to the fire, and Jeff went back to his chair. I couldn't find a comfortable spot anywhere because here it was. Brian began to read the fourth story. I could not bear to watch, but I was too miserable to look away. I had no more hope.

Brian read, stopped. He looked startled, momentarily confused, then began to laugh. "How did you manage this? Sly. It's amazing." He flipped through the pages. "In just your style, too."

To my relief and joy, he tossed the story aside and began the next one. Jeff, the dummy, wouldn't let it pass.

"Manage what? Which story?" he asked. Now it was his turn to look confused.

Brian looked up. "Oh, manage? Manage to slip in 'Low Hurdles.' Good gag. Guess you filched a copy of it when you were up to see me last time. Unless *you* wrote it and gave it to my student, who passed it off on me. When I think of his other work, which was merely okay—not bad, but not great—that explanation is the more likely one, except that I don't think you'd cheat."

At this point I began whispering furiously to Jeff, "Yes, yes. Joke. Laugh. I'll explain later." But no, he wouldn't listen.

Later Jeff knew he should have kept quiet and thought it out alone, but at the time he got too hot and blurted out, "That's nobody else's story. I wrote it last fall. I didn't give it to anyone or take it from anyone."

"Come on," laughed Brian. "I have read exactly this story last fall, submitted by a student. Gave him an A."

"Exactly? Word for word or similar idea?" demanded Jeff.

"Exactly the same format, style, maybe some words

different, but not that many," Brian sighed.

"Well, I didn't steal. I don't plagiarize," announced Jeff somewhat stiffly.

Brian shrugged. "I can get a copy from the student to show you. The only other thing I can think of is that both of you heard it or read it somewhere a while back and coincidentally came up with it again, but that is very farfetched. There would be more differences. You're sure you're not just having me on, Jeff?"

"No, I'm serious."

Brian hardly seemed to glance at the rest of the folder. Why should he, thought Jeff. If one is stolen, then why not all. The whole evening seemed to collapse.

"I don't know. I don't understand," Brian said. "I'm beat. I'll call you tomorrow. G'night, kid. Thanks."

He was gone.

Morosely, Jeff cleaned up, wound the clock, closed up the house, and went to bed.

When Brian had written that he was expected to live at the graduate college while he taught the seminar, Jeff had been disappointed. But Brian had driven down early so they could spend time together. Now it was ruined, ruined. Jeff wished he had used his school vacation to go skiing with his parents rather than hang around to see his hero cousin. Jeff swore. I told him that I had tried to persuade him to go skiing instead, but he still wasn't listening.

Jeff slept badly and awoke early. He went out to run. The first five miles went by without a single thought; down to the lake, around the lake, back up the hill toward home, each footfall a squeaking crunch on the snow. Back home he did sit-ups, push-ups, any old exercises until he was totally bored. He showered, dressed, made himself a big breakfast, and ate without pleasure. After he had cleaned up the kitchen, he chanced a look at the clock. By now he must have killed most of the morning. The clock stood at nine.

His math class at the university didn't begin until one o'clock. Glumly, Jeff wandered into the living room and sat down at the piano. He played for an hour, refusing to answer the telephone, which rang once.

Brian used his one break that morning to make some telephone calls. He asked a librarian friend with a good computer to look for a story like "Low Hurdles." He called someone who could find the student who'd given him "Low Hurdles" last fall. Brian called Jeff. No answer.

Many days went by, all of them bad ones for Jeff. He wrote nothing, did no homework to speak of, and avoided Brian. For the most part, I made myself scarce. It occurred to me to try to talk to Jeff, to tell him some plausible story, to explain it all, and I did come up with one or two rather good ones. Finally, however, I rejected them and just waited.

One day Jeff came home to find a copy of his story in the mailbox. I watched while he opened it. Since I'd kept quiet all this time, it seemed wise to wait a bit longer, until he had digested it all before I tried once more to help him out of his mess.

Jeff read the story. It was his story, but not his. The title was the same, with here and there a different word, just the way people change things when they steal, or when they don't have an especially good ear. One thing was exactly the same. The date typed on the paper.

Jeff sat down at his desk. By now he wondered if he *had* stolen or somehow written a story he had heard. But two people writing the same story on the same day?

At this point I concentrated all my strength on making myself visible. I'd never done it before, and wasn't even sure I could, but somehow I felt it would be more impressive. I wanted Jeff to let me stay with him. I liked him; he was talented, very talented. We could do great things together if he would not throw me out. I thought I had made myself visible, but Jeff still ignored me. I wasn't certain that I could remain visible and talk at the same time, but I tried.

"Ahem. Pardon me. I think I can help you. All you have to do is tell your cousin that it was a bad joke and you're sorry and tell your editor to scratch the story because you have a better one. We can write that one now . . . if you're not too busy," I added apologetically. He didn't answer.

"Or you could tell Brian that you have ESP and transmitted the story while you were writing it. You didn't know your power or how to use it yet—first attempt, you know—and you tried to send it to him. You thought he hadn't got it at all and were surprised the student got it. Or you could say that—"

"Wait a minute," Jeff nearly shouted, and I was right next to him. "What are these ideas?" he demanded, looking at me in a way I didn't like at all.

"I was merely trying to help you out of the mess you are in." I was a little bit offended.

"Mess I'm in! I'll say. Just how did I get into this mess?"

"Ah," said I. "If you'll just let me explain." I could feel that the enormous effort to remain visible was simply too much for me. I began to fade, so I started to talk quite rapidly so that Jeff wouldn't think I'd run away.

"You do know who I am?" I continued. I couldn't help sighing in relief as I ceased being visible.

"Not really. I recognize your voice. . . ."

"I have the honor to be your muse. I was assigned to you shortly before you—that is, before *we*—wrote 'Low Hurdles,' which is excellent. I've learned so much about sports since coming to you, and you really are quite a gifted writer. You will go far—"

"Muse?" he interrupted me again. I think he was disappointed that I was not a sweet young girl, instead of a mature—

"You look like an aged urchin and you seem more interested in making trouble than in inspiring my writing."

I was shocked. "Why, Jeff! I've never known you to be rude. What is the matter?"

"Matter? My cousin and I are not speaking. He thinks I am a thief. I've got to call back a story I know I wrote, and you just fill the air with words. Why, I don't even know how many other stories of mine you've messed up, given to a hundred or so well-chosen people or taken from I don't know where. How many of my stories have you—"

"Jeff, Jeff. Please, I swear it is just that one story that is . . . er, well, messed up."

"Now," he was shouting again, "just tell me straight out. Precisely how were those two stories written on the same night?"

I cleared my throat. Dry, this steam heat. Jeff got up and began to walk around the house, just the way he does when we are working together. I felt better when he did that.

"As I said," I began, trotting along after him so that I would not need to shout, "I did not know you very well. I did not know that your cousin taught at that little backwater college. I did not even know that I could send your story out as I did. I was just trying . . . that is, I was trying because that poor guy was sweating away with no talent and I just . . . His fraternity brothers talked him into taking the course for a joke, and his mother was sick, and his sister a shoplifter, and—"

"How come you know so much about that guy? Were you his muse?"

"Well, no, I wasn't. I'm just telling you what I *think* were the details of his life. I was also," I added, knowing that it sounded a bit lame, "well, I confess I *was* guilty of testing my powers. I did it to see if I could do it, and out of pity for someone who was, if you will, sweating a course. No one will know. Actually," I added quickly, "that guy is not even going to be a writer. He's—"

"I may not either!"

Once again I was glad Jeff could not see me.

"You," I said, "you have talent. With me to inspire you, you'll be one of the greats. As soon as we clear up this difficulty, you—we—can get to work."

"What," said Jeff in a voice so low I could hardly hear him, "what if I don't want to work with you? What if I complain? What if I get you recalled?"

"Jeff, you *wouldn't!*" I tried not to plead. "You might not get another, or you might get a weak one, or a poor one. Besides I won't do it again. I promise."

"Have you been a muse for anyone other than me?"

"No. Yes. Well, actually I am very, very old. Oh, I don't want to talk about it."

" 'No. Yes.' You don't want to talk about it. Great! Now what do I do? You could be a disaster for me."

"So could a different muse," I replied with dignity. "We all have our little faults. Your cousin's muse isn't perfect either. I could tell you stories. . . ."

"I'll bet you could," Jeff sighed. He wouldn't listen to me anymore. These days of anxiety had worn me out, too. I went off to take a nap.

When I returned, he was back at his desk. I said hello; he looked at his watch.

"Where have you been? I have been working for an hour. Come on, muse, let's go."

When I tried to find out what he'd done, he said he had canceled the story and told his cousin—of all things—the truth. He said he did not understand how the whole thing had happened. I like that. He also told his cousin that he was sorry for getting angry with him, and that he had to decide whether or not to keep on writing.

I guess I am on probation.

The Storytellers

It all began, as so many things do, with a quarrel—
something quite unusual in those placid days. At that time,
the earth was a smooth, quiet green ball, with here and there a
few trees that provided some shade from the sun, which
shone all the time. The people who lived on the earth in those
days had little to do. They liked nothing better than to gather
under those trees to listen to stories. Storytellers roamed the
earth, telling their tales to groups of willing listeners. The
stories were pleasant enough, but they were as dull as the life
on that smooth green ball.

Now it happened one day that a bent and toothless old
storyteller came to a grove of trees just as another storyteller,
who herself seemed to be a grandmother of some years, was
spinning a tale before a delighted audience. The old one
stopped to listen, then began to shake and to stamp her feet.

"You! You!" she called. "You have stolen my story."

"I have not!" retorted the other hotly. "I heard this story
when I was but a girl. I heard it from a young woman who told
it then."

"Ah hah! You see? I told you so. I was that young woman.
The story is mine!" shouted the old crone gleefully.

Such dissension was something quite new. In no time at
all the listeners joined in the shouting. Soon the original
quarrel was lost in claims and counterclaims about every
story that had ever been told and everyone had a headache
from the quarreling. In a lull someone suggested that they
hold a storytelling contest to decide who was the greatest
among the storytellers.

It was done. Criers went everywhere announcing the

contest that was to be held, with stories old and new, told by tellers from all over the face of the smooth, quiet, green earth. On the day of the contest, all the storytellers and all the listeners gathered together. Of course, good as they were, the two old women with whom it had all begun were not among the greatest tellers. The contest continued, as one after another the stories were spun out for that vast gathering. The quarrel had let loose something new upon the earth. The stories got better and better as time went on. Finally, there remained just three tellers.

All the people fell into an expectant hush as the first of the three strode forward. He was young and strong, of medium height, with gray eyes that gave off sparks as he spoke. Standing before them with his sturdy legs planted firmly on the quiet green earth, he began a tale of injustice, of monstrous cruelty, of the yoke of slavery, of the lash, of babies torn from their mothers' arms.

And as he spoke of outrage upon outrage, the listeners said, "Ah-h-h-h . . . oh-h-h-h . . ." and struck their thighs with clenched fists. As the horrors mounted, the young people jumped up and cried out, "Stop them! We must stop them. We must free the captives!"

Indeed, the very earth no longer slumbered. She, too, listened and, like the people, was filled with fury, with a desire for revenge. The earth trembled, shook, moved, and then rose up. Mountains formed with a terrible crack, rumble, and roar. The people stared in awe. The mountains stood shimmering around them as the storyteller brought his tale to its dreadful conclusion.

At first there was silence. People shivered in the shadows cast by the mountains. Then followed murmurs of admiration for this powerful teller of tales. Looking at the mountains, the people were afraid of their beauty and their might.

It was a long while before the next storyteller stepped forward. She was tall and slender, with hair of silver and gold. Her gentle face was beautiful and a little sad. In a soft voice she began a story of love, of such joy, tenderness, pain, and sorrow that the people listened in complete silence, with tears streaming down their faces. As she told on and on, she brought smiles and nods of agreement, and among the listeners, gentle, affectionate looks were given one to another.

She told them a story of the beginning of love, the fullness of love, the betrayal of love, the death of love, and of the loneliness of those without love.

The earth, once awakened, could not contain herself, and she, too, wept for love. The waters poured forth. The people were once more astonished, this time to see oceans, lakes, and rivers appear.

And the young people were filled with a longing to travel on those oceans and to climb those mountains. As they waited for the third storyteller to appear, they chewed upon nuts and spat out the shells and drew pictures of boats upon the sand, and a desire for adventure came over them.

Finally the third storyteller appeared. A tiny, thin old man hobbled out with the aid of a staff much taller than he. His black eyes were merry, his voice full of mischief. He made the people chuckle with tales of the tricksters, of the clever cheats. Babies snuggled in their mothers' arms. Small children curled up and smiled, delighting in each clever trick, nodding in agreement with every wise choice, softly repeating the words to themselves.

As the old man went from tale to tale, the crowd sighed. The sun, who had so long shone always without rest, slowly sank below the horizon. The old man crooned his tales and the people smiled as they drifted off to sleep. The children peeped out from beneath their lashes to see, for the very first time, twinkling above them the stars in the nighttime sky.

"Ah, look! Pictures in the sky!"

As the children slept they dreamed of the stories those starry pictures told, and of the adventures they themselves would have on the vast oceans and jagged peaks. And as they slept, the old storyteller smiled and hobbled away to where he, too, could take his rest.

And who was the greatest of the three storytellers? No one could say.

A Little Love Story

The man sitting at the large untidy desk put the last of a small pile of papers into a manila folder and closed it. He stared out the window absentmindedly for a moment, then glanced at his watch. With practiced movements, he smoothed his thick, nearly snow-white hair into place before he pushed back his chair and rose to his feet. Glancing at a large clock on the wall and then at his wristwatch, he left the room, turning off the light behind him. In the corridor he greeted two silver-haired women as they passed, then turned and walked into a door marked "Studio A."

After exchanging greetings with the others in the room, he sat down behind another desk and opened his folder. A moment or so later, he received his "On the air" signal and began to speak.

"Good evening, ladies and gentlemen. This is Edward Craig with the Evening Information Service." Then calmly, unhurriedly, he gave a brief account of the international agreements signed that day, of the value of the major world currencies, of a fire in the city that afternoon that had blazed briefly and been put out with no injuries and little damage.

Throughout his account, he was articulate, calm, and as accurate as possible. There was no attempt to seem "sympathetic," no inflation of a news item; the broadcast was exactly what it was called, an information service. Finally the manila folder was empty. The man paused a few seconds, then continued in a voice that was quite subdued.

"Today we had expected our World Census Data Bank to tell us that one hundred percent of the world's population had reached age sixty. We would have then given you a more complete breakdown of the census figures. Instead we have learned that the census bank has received a report that there are four people in the world who are fifteen years old." He paused again. "It seems logical to assume that if there are four young people who are accounted for, then there are quite possibly more. Governments all over the earth are now attempting to learn whether there are more of the young people, who were, long ago, called teenagers." He cleared his throat and went on.

"You will recall that for quite a few years we assumed that any children born would appear in what were once the heavily populated regions of Asia, India, or South America. Searches conducted there proved fruitless. We had forgotten the awesome efficiency of the bombs used in the last war, bombs that removed inhabitants without scratching the furniture. Those regions were devastated and have remained even more sparsely populated than our own; the record keeping has been, thus far, quite accurate. These four young people have appeared in North America.

"You may ask what their presence means. Possibly nothing. Their number is so very small. We shall see. Until our next report, then, good night."

"Off the air" flashed. The man wiped his forehead with a handkerchief. A pleasant-looking woman entered the room and waited next to the door. She shifted a briefcase, which was obviously heavy, from one hand to the other. The man crossed the room to her.

"Nan, I'm so glad you could come."

"Ted, I don't think I've ever seen you so disturbed."

He did not reply, just kissed her lightly on the cheek and reached for the briefcase.

"What's in there?"

"Work," she replied.

They left the studio and proceeded down the corridor without speaking. Nan opened the door to an office, the same one Ted had left just half an hour earlier. She went in and sat down in one of two large armchairs facing the desk.

"Will you drink coffee or tea?" he asked as he put down the briefcase, walked to a cabinet in one corner of the room, and touched a button. The room filled with the low, smooth sounds of fine old jazz. Nan smiled.

"Coffee, please."

"Me, too. Smells good," Ted replied, returning to the desk with two cups. He sat down in the other armchair.

For a few minutes neither one spoke.

"When I was a little boy," Ted began, "the grown-ups told a story. I think it was about my grandfather or great-grandfather. Anyway, when he was two, or perhaps even younger, he saw a picture—in a book I still have—of a dinosaur lying on ferns and grass. The text said something like, 'No one knows why the dinosaurs became extinct,' but my grandfather couldn't read the text. He saw the picture and said, quite logically, 'Dinosaur sleeping.' Neither of his sisters, nor his parents, had the heart to tell him anything else. I've often thought of that picture and wondered whether the dinosaurs just got tired . . ."

"And?" Nan asked.

"Now these children. I wonder about them."

"So do I," she replied.

"I wonder whether they are energetic, and whether they are going to be warlike."

Nan laughed. "Four of them could hardly do much that way."

Ted nodded his agreement. "Yes, but I mean, is our race more mature or are we only peaceful because we are few and we are old?"

Nan looked up from her cup, but before she could speak, Ted continued.

"I wonder, too, whether they are sterile."

"As far as I know not one of them is a clone."

"So I have heard, but still they might be sterile."

"True," Nan whispered. She looked at Ted for quite a long time before she lowered her eyes and took another drink from her cup.

"You know, I had seen myself as a historian turned newscaster, reporting the demise of our kind. Each species with its time on earth, and man one of them, one who foolishly wasted his gifts, etcetera, etcetera." He spread his hands before him in the air in a gesture of dispersion. He stood up, took both cups, and refilled them. Putting them on the desk, he walked over to the window and looked out.

"I keep going over the history of it all, wondering whether these," he paused, "these teenagers know about it. Do they know how sometime in the late nineteen hundreds grandparents began to show a strong preference for receiving a nicely retouched studio portrait once a year rather than a visit from living, most probably unruly, grandchildren. Then how people began to choose not to have or not to raise children for various reasons, and how the clone nurseries seemed to work so well. Still, everything seemed fine until that day when all the old lessons about war were forgotten. After that there were so few people left, and the clones were sterile, and . . ."

"Sterile in the oddest way," mused Nan over the rim of her cup. "All systems present, all worked for cloning but not for 'normal' reproduction. And each successive clone of a clone turned out to be less intelligent, less energetic, weaker in all ways, as if the genetic code had a built-in block against cloning."

Ted returned to his chair. "So here we are. It had seemed to me that we humans were, one by one, settling down on the grass to go to sleep. Now I wonder."

"Would you like to meet them?" she asked.

"The children? The young people? Very much! But I don't understand. Does your Institute have something to do with them?"

"The Institute! Most definitely not, but they would like to. That is just one of the problems." She looked up at the clock on the office wall. "It's rather a long story, but I can tell you a bit before we leave for the train. I was on my way over here to see you when I got your message asking me to come by. I had wanted to tell you before the story became public, but some things got in the way and I couldn't get here in time.

"I reported the existence of the children to the World Census Data Bank. The children asked me to do it as part of their own search for others their age. And," she continued before Ted could speak, "one of the children is mine."

"Yours?"

"Yes. Not telling is a very old habit, one difficult to break. My husband and I simply made it a practice not to mention our child to anyone who was not naturally a part of our family life. People in the village knew, thought it an aberration, and never said much. When the children—each of them grew up in isolation—asked if there were others, it turned out that a very loose network did indeed exist. People knew people who knew people who knew of a child. That is how they found one another.

"While our child was growing up, my husband and I could indulge ourselves and talk of Annie with one another, thereby sparing those who could not possibly be interested. Another reason for saying nothing had to do with the attitudes of some people.

"You may recall Woodrow, the head of our Institute. He has been searching for years for a breeding population to save the human race from extinction. He is quite mad. Once the Census Bank had my report, Woodrow was informed immediately and began to make plans to 'protect' the children from all the normal dangers one encounters growing up and to keep them in a sort of laboratory zoo. He wants to appeal to their idealism to convince them to repopulate the earth. Once he discovers that one of the children is mine he'll give me no peace. Hence my arm-breaking briefcase. I am going home to work. There will be no more Institute for me." She paused for breath.

"Please don't be hurt. Really, parents can be quite tedious about their offspring. And then, we were no longer young when Annie was born. You must realize how very strange our having a child would have seemed to people. After my husband died, I continued my away-from-home silence, even after you and I became friends. I know it must seem strange. . . ."

"I'd better pack if we are going to make the train." Ted stood up and put his cup on the desk.

An hour or so later, the train pulled out of the tunnel that ran under the river. Nan gestured toward the window and sighed.

"It's always so beautiful."

The green forests of New Jersey grew all the way to the water's edge. The train moved placidly up the steep grade. Ted nodded agreement and pointed to a restaurant, nearly hidden by the trees at the top of the cliff.

"We haven't eaten there in quite a while. The food used to be good and the view superb."

"Yes. But I've heard they closed."

"Ah, I remember now. The chef was ninety-two and having trouble finding an assistant."

The train left the forest and passed through a stretch of open countryside beyond which were two rather large farms.

"Have you ever seen the films of this area when it was city and suburb all the way from New York to Philadelphia?" Ted asked.

"Yes, once. It was years ago in an undergraduate history course."

They were silent, each watching out of the train windows as once again they entered the shade of a forest.

"These children. What can you tell me about them?" he asked.

"In a way, I'd rather have you see for yourself." Nan paused, then laughed. "One thing about them I can tell you because you won't see it. It has already changed."

"What's that?"

"One of the boys, Keith, arrived here with his grandfather, who walks with a pronounced limp. Keith limped in with his grandfather. I only realized later, when I saw Keith's walk after the children had been together a few days, that

Annie, too, had unconsciously matched her walk to mine. It just dawned on me that now they all walk—well, swagger might be too strong, but they move like one another. There are individual differences which you will see. But before knowing one another, each one had walked like a much older person."

The cracked voice of the trainman came through the loudspeakers. "Next stop, Princeton."

They alighted from the train and walked through the tiny village, stopping once to buy some fresh strawberries from an old lady sitting on her porch. Nan and the old lady chatted for a moment or two about events in the village before she and Ted continued their walk.

At last they entered a house just outside the village. Inside it was cool, dark, and quiet. A note lay on the hall table. Nan scanned it quickly.

"They have all gone camping with Rachel and her parents. They'll be back tomorrow about noon." She looked up at him. "I hope you're not too disappointed."

Ted leaned forward and kissed her. "No, I'm not. Shall I cook or assist?"

The following morning Ted arose at dawn and left the house quietly. He walked rapidly down to the river, across the bridge, through the forest on the opposite side, then back up a hill to what had once been a great university. Now it was a museum of sorts, with a library and other facilities for the few who still pursued research there. Forty years earlier, his class had been quite small, and it had been the last one to graduate from this university, or any other.

Without thinking, Ted slowed his pace, which was a mistake. He had begun to sweat from what had been a walk of nearly five miles at a very fast pace, and within minutes he felt a bit chilled.

The old stone dormitories had already been empty shells when he studied there. Now his footsteps echoed through them, as they had echoed through medieval monasteries in Europe and in the shells of universities all over the world.

84

Four young people. Would they want to start a new world? Even if they did, would they be enough to start the human race once again? He laughed at himself.

"Adam and Eve were just two," he said aloud, then was startled by the hollow echo of his words.

Now thoroughly chilled, Ted walked quickly back to the house outside the village. He showered, shaved, and dressed.

Nan was on the terrace, reading. Massaging his shoulder, which felt unpleasantly sore, he walked over to her and gently touched her hair. She looked up.

"Did I ever tell you," he began abruptly, "that my wife and I would have had a child the same age as these?"

"No," she replied, putting down her book, "you didn't."

"When she died, she was pregnant. The accident killed them both, for the baby was too small to survive on its own. That is one of the many reasons I am so interested in these children."

"I hope you won't be disappointed. But, then, I don't know what you expect."

"Neither do I. Many of my questions are, shall we say, historical, and I probably won't live to see the answers."

"Like so many of our questions," she replied. She watched a squirrel approach a bed of tulips and select a red one. Carefully, he clipped off the flower and, petal by petal, ate it.

"I had something I wanted to tell you. I was thinking that Woodrow had irritated me so that I became unreasonably concerned for the children's freedom. I began to imagine how ridiculous it would be, a group of octogenarian guards for a group of healthy young people. Woodrow is, if you will pardon the expression, a toothless tiger. What can he *do* if the children want to live normally, to take risks—put them in a cage?"

> I see the moon,
> The moon sees me.
> The moon sees the one
> I long to see.

> So God bless the moon,
> And God bless me,
> And God bless the one
> I long to see.
>
> I had a heart forever true . . .

The song, sung loudly and somewhat off-key, preceeded a rickety old minibus as it creaked along the streets of the village. At every house, those that were not abandoned ruins, doors or windows flew open. From each one peered a face, wrinkled, with hair gone white or gone entirely. Each look was followed by a smile and a shrug, and each head slowly disappeared inside. One woman paused to address her neighbor.

"Of course it could only be them, but somehow I always forget."

Both women laughed and returned the waves they received from the open windows of the lumbering bus.

By the time the bus finally sighed and coughed to a stop, Nan and Ted stood in front of the house. It was long after noon, and Nan had clearly been worried. The door of the bus opened and a girl jumped out. She ran to her mother and threw her arms around her as she spoke rapidly, breathlessly.

"Sorry we were so late, no way to telephone. The bus broke down continually, but Keith always fixed it. He knows all about fossil fuels, postfossil fuels, motors and engines of every sort, everything that works or could work. He even has a passing acquaintance with horses and mules. The forest was great. We want to go back—" She stopped suddenly when she saw Ted.

Ted did not notice. He was too surprised to do more than stare, first at the bus as it disgorged more people: a boy with unnaturally shiny hair combed up on the sides and down in the middle, wearing pants very small at the ankles and ballooning at his slim hips; then a girl—slender, so fragile that she seemed almost transparent—bearing an enormous backpack; next, another boy, his hands black with grease, his face serious, smudged with oil. Last to emerge were a man and woman, both very fit. To Ted, who had spent time in both desert and mountains, they were clearly people who knew the woods and spent time there.

Ted hardly knew where to look or to listen. He barely heard Nan when she spoke.

"Annie, I have told you about my friend, Ted. Ted, this is my daughter, Annie."

Finally Ted took hold of himself and offered the girl his hand.

"Hello, Annie. I'm very glad to meet you. I'm simply thunderstruck at—forgive me—at how beautiful you are, and at how much you two look alike."

Neither Annie nor Nan could reply. The other campers surged around them and everyone went inside the house.

The remainder of the afternoon, the dinner, the whole evening that followed, were so intense, so charged with excitement as the children developed ideas for a "grand project," that Ted awoke the next morning with a slight hangover.

Once again, he went out to walk and think. When he returned, he tried to write it all down. Yesterday he had been hurt that Nan had never told him about her child, but he did not, could not, pursue the slight. Things were moving too rapidly.

Late that day he returned to Manhattan to pack and to resign.

The head of the network, a man who had, in his years, attained half the height and twice the girth of Ted, puffed on his cigar, ran his thick fingers over his bald pate, and sighed.

"Crazy. But sounds like fun. Wish I'd been invited to go along. These—what do they call themselves again?"

"The Four Musketeers. Annie, who has read just about everything, suggested it as apt. Then Danny—he's the one who grew up in Hollywood—seconded it. He said he's seen at least five movie versions of the old Dumas novel, including one or two set in the space age, which comment led Keith— he's the one from the farm who can fix anything—to ask why we had given up exploring space. Then they all turned to me as resident historian, and I recited what I knew: how with so few people after the war, and an aging population, people abandoned most of the earth, drastically limited air travel, and have since concentrated on just keeping things going as best they can. 'We're waiting for space to visit us,' I told them.

"Then the conversation turned to seeing the world. The children want to see it all and they want to go together, to share their individual pasts, their knowledge, their passions, if you will, with one another. No two have had the same experiences.

"Rachel and her parents, for example, have lived a very isolated life, mainly doing math and music and acquiring a solid knowledge of how to live self-sufficiently in the forest. Everyone loved this glimpse of the forest, so now it is on for more. And Keith wants everyone to see his parents' farm. He can make something, some sort of bus, go. They want to travel the old highways, follow the wagon-train route across North America."

"Sounds suspiciously like *Swiss Family Robinson*, if you ask me," puffed the head of the network through his cigar.

"Exactly," Ted agreed and continued. "Annie, with all her bookish knowledge, is also a natural storyteller; her mother is, you may recall, a biologist. They plan to hit all the old universities on our journey.

"When we get to Hollywood, Danny wants to show us lots of movies, millions of them, I think. He told us that at some point he tried to see all of them, like someone reading his way through the library, but he got stuck on favorites, which he watched again and again. He grew up playing in the old studios, where he said they have warehouses of costumes and clothes collected after the bombs. Danny also said that his mother had blue hair, nails, lips, eyes, and glasses! He says everyone out there looks different, different from us, from one another, and from himself or herself!"

"Can't even imagine it," replied the head of the network, puffing slowly.

What Ted did not tell his old friend was how Annie, in her direct way, had come over to him at one point and said, "Ted, we all want you to come along with us." She shrugged and plunged on. "I know it would be a crazy sort of honeymoon for you and Mother. I mean . . . that is if you two had planned . . . Well, what I want to say is that Mother and I have mourned Father. Now we should live the way we did when he was alive, the way he would want us to live." She began to falter, "The way we can now." She looked away, then fled, embarrassed at her outburst.

Later Ted tried unsuccessfully to catch Annie's eye. He wanted to tell her that she had not backed herself into proposing that he marry her mother. He and Nan had already discussed their future at some length. Later, when he talked with Nan, she promised to reassure Annie.

"I think she was concerned for me, now that she has a rather exciting life ahead of her, one we never imagined. She is growing away from me, even though she wants me on the trip, at least at first. She wants to be sure she is not abandoning me."

Ted sat silent, mentally retracing the events and conversations of the past two days. The head of the network coughed once or twice, louder each time. Ted started.

"Sorry. What were you saying?"

The head of the network removed his cigar and stared at it for a moment before he began.

"I was just thinking of when you and I were students together some forty years ago, remembering that story you told me about your grandfather. I was wondering . . . wondering if the dinosaurs are asleep."

Minnie

Minnie waxes with adversity and wanes with comfort and ease. She is strong, caring, and terribly competent when disaster strikes, and suffers in sloth when life is smooth. For most of her life, she has simply been near, ready to help when trouble arose, but somehow along the line, Minnie's patience wore thin. Waiting was insufficient.

For a long time I was too much in love with Minnie to notice just how frequently disaster accompanied her, just how often I had heard her say, "No, no. No payment, thank you." She'd speak softly and blush a bit, most becomingly. "I only wanted to help." Minnie always said these things and meant them. She could then bask in everyone's gratitude.

Did I say that Minnie needs adversity? Ah, yes, and she also needs gratitude. I have seen Minnie wish for an automobile accident, and for specific injuries, so that she could save someone before the rescue squad could arrive. Minnie on the spot. I have seen Minnie cause infections, diseases, and fires, simply by wishing for them. Later I learned that Minnie never had been entirely above helping things along. When she was a child, she mastered quite early the techniques for surreptitiously teasing a younger child until it howled, then rushing to comfort it so that she earned rich praises.

Yes, yes. I know it sounds incredible. For a while I, too, refused to believe it. Then, when I could no longer ignore what was happening, I still didn't tell anyone. Now I can't.

Once I realized what Minnie was doing, I should have cut and run. Instead, like a sap, I tried to persuade Minnie to stop using her powers. I asked her to join me in some sort of normal life.

"Let's get married, have five or six kids. Just in the regular course of life, with no help from you, those kids will generate enough sickness, accidents, and general chaos to satisfy even *your* need for disaster, Minnie." I even laughed. You see, I thought she loved me.

I'll never forget the look on Minnie's face; it was fear. Not just because I knew. No. It took me a moment to realize just what it was. Minnie could enjoy herself only when she didn't get involved, when she didn't care. Her act was for strangers, for her public. She didn't want anything at all to do with loving someone or something and having it in danger. Minnie did not need appreciation or gratitude from a husband or family who loved her. No, no thrill there, no basking in the gratitude on the faces of strangers, no admiration from an appreciative public. I had asked her to be vulnerable. That was too much.

"How brave she is, how cheerful, what sacrifice," say the neighbors, the newspapers, every passerby. "He's helpless, you know, paralyzed," they whisper, "in nappies, unable to speak, and so young. Poor Minnie, what devotion. He was stricken before they could even marry. Why, he could live for years."

That's what scares me the most, that "He could live for years." Apparently Minnie decided she needed a long-term project. I am that project. I am completely in Minnie's power. I can only try to will her to decide that the world's undying admiration will reward her even more if I recover—that is, she "recovers" me. I wonder if my will is strong enough, wonder how threatened Minnie still feels. If Minnie gets bored or decides her life is now too confining, it's curtains for me. Which would mean even more love and sympathy for brave Minnie.

My situation is hopeless. I cannot possibly escape, even if I do recover. How could I ever leave my intended bride, the girl who cared for me when I was struck down?

Minnie doesn't tell me what's on her mind; she just tends me.

"If I Had the Wings of an Angel"

The lock gave with a soft click. It was so easy. Chickie opened the door slowly, just a crack. No chain. He listened. Not a sound came from the apartment. Opening the door just enough to squeeze past, he slipped inside. Once more he listened, his heart pounding. Can't be too careful, not on your first job. A refrigerator hummed. Through the open window, he could hear street noises; otherwise the apartment was silent. The room was lit by an old-fashioned floor lamp with a stained yellow shade, down at the far end of the living room, next to a shabby armchair.

Chickie looked. Nothing here. He needed small stuff, money would be best, tape deck, something to sell. The room was full of books, bookcases on both walls, books on tables. Can't sell books, thought Chickie with disgust. Closing the door behind him, he went to the bedroom and opened the door slowly. It was dark inside, but after a few seconds his eyes adjusted, and the light from the living room was enough for him to see the dresser. Great, thought Chickie, an ashtray full of change, a wallet.

Intent on the money, Chickie darted across the room. When the old man spoke, Chickie nearly dropped dead from fright. "Water ... please," rasped a voice from the floor. Chickie had almost stepped on him. When Chickie bent down, the smell hit him. "Water ... " repeated the old man. Only his lips moved when he spoke.

He's sick, thought Chickie. The bathroom door was straight ahead. Chickie found the glass, filled it, and returned to the old man, who had not stirred.

Gently supporting the old man's head, Chickie gave him

water, trying meanwhile to hold his breath. The smell was awful. Some of the water spilled, but the old man sipped slowly, swallowed.

"You sick?" asked Chickie.

"Stroke," whispered the old man. "Days ago. Can't move."

"If I lift you, can you? Geeze, you're a mess! C'mon old man, we've gotta clean you up."

While the bathtub filled, Chickie peeled off the old man's clothes, retching all the while. Covering the old man with a sheet from the bed, he took the clothes, rolled them in newspaper from a stack in the kitchen, and took them out to the incinerator chute in the hall, completely forgetting to watch for neighbors or the police.

Using towels from the bathroom, Chickie washed the old man as well as he could, then lifted him into the tub and washed him again. Once the old man was clean, dressed in pajamas, and sitting in bed, Chickie sat down. His own clothes were soaked.

"Hey, old man, you need something to eat."

"Tea, toast," rasped the old man. "Thanks."

Chickie returned to the kitchen. It was very neat, very clean, not much in the cupboards, but what Chickie liked most of all were a washer and dryer standing one on top of the other near the kitchen window. Chuckie admired them for a moment, then found what he needed and carried it to the old man.

"Hungry, kid?" whispered the old man when Chickie returned. "Eat," he commanded.

"Yeah, I'll eat," said Chickie. "You got a great place, Pops."

"Sheets—in—closet by—front door. Make up—couch," answered the old man, speaking very slowly, as if each word were an enormous effort.

Chickie fed him, then cleaned up the crumbs.

"Medicine," commanded the old man.

Chickie found the pills on the bedside table, amidst more books, and gave him the ones he indicated.

"Thanks, kid. Eat. Sleep."

Chickie turned off the bedroom light and returned to the kitchen, where he threw the towels and sheets into the washer with some bleach, and turned it on. Must be great stuff, watching your own things get clean in your own washer. There seemed to be enough room, so Chickie added his own clothes.

Chickie ate. He washed his dishes, dried them, and put them away. It was great to have such control, to know you'd put something somewhere and find it there later, to walk into the kitchen and have it look the same; two other rooms, both that way, and a bathroom.

Chickie took a shower, found some sheets, and made up the couch. It was so easy to pretend that this place was his. As he turned out the light, he looked up. What a lot of books, wonder if he's read all of them, thought Chickie. That reminded him of the old man, and he couldn't sleep till he had checked on him. The old man slept peacefully. Reassured, Chickie returned to the couch where he, too, slept.

Chickie awoke once, feeling very scared. He heard the old man calling desperately, "Kid! Hurry! Toilet!" Chickie ran; they made it. The remainder of the night was quiet.

The next morning Chickie was up early. Feeling luxurious, he took another shower. The old man seemed stronger. His speech was clearer and words came more easily. Chickie carried him out to the living room and put him in the armchair. Chickie made him breakfast and fed him, carefully wiping the dribbles of egg from the old man's chin.

"Need a shave, Pops," laughed Chickie.

"I'll grow a beard," replied the old man.

"Good idea, don't think I could do it," laughed Chickie again.

He hummed to himself, "Mood so high, feel I could fly." No reason to feel so great. As a burglar he hadn't made it last night; instead he was babysitting for an old man. Crazy.

After breakfast Chickie cleaned up the kitchen. The old man seemed impatient and began giving Chickie orders before Chickie was done.

"What's up, Pops?"

"We don't have much time, and I want to get started. I gotta at least learn what we have to do."

"Whaddya mean?" asked Chickie, wiping his hands on the towel.

"We gotta keep you out of jail. I can do it, but I don't have much time."

"Jail?" laughed Chickie. "Me? How?"

"Yeah, jail. You're headed there now. But I think we can avoid it. I'll do it using these." He looked at the shelves of books. "We'll get you in a good school, get you an education. Now let's see what you know besides picking locks."

"School! Man, I hate school. It's a drag. Noise, the smell, guys beating you up, taking your money. I hate school."

"Yeah. Well, jail's just like it, only worse. No, we'll get you in a good school. Come on."

The old man went to work on Chickie, finding out just what he knew. While he asked questions, he had Chickie massage his arms, especially the right one. "I gotta write," he rasped in his hoarse whisper. Chickie worked on the old man's thin arms and the old man worked over the bare spots in Chickie's education. Finally, the old man ordered Chickie to stop. Never in Chickie's life had a morning passed so quickly.

"Take some money. Get us some food." The old man then dictated a list. Chickie wrote laboriously. "No soda, no junk, at least for a while. We gotta get you in shape."

"Me? I'm in great shape," Chickie replied incredulously.

"We'll see," said the old man. "And you need a change of clothes."

Chickie went out to shop. He was worried about cops and storekeepers and neighbors. School had started two weeks ago, so the truant officers would be out, too. Chickie jumped whenever anyone spoke to him. When he was finished, he found a phone booth that worked and called his mother. He needed lots of change by the time the woman who lived downstairs yelled up to his mother and his mother yelled down, and his mother finally got on the phone and yelled at him.

"Girl? You with a girl? You'll get in trouble, too. No good, like the rest of them!"

It took a lot more change to say he wouldn't be back for a while.

When Chickie returned, the old man seemed to be dozing in his chair, but he sat up, quite alert, when Chickie came near him. After lunch they worked again, then the old man told Chickie to take down one book, then another and another. One was a novel, another a biography, a third a book of exercises.

"Read these first," ordered the old man.

"Say," said Chickie, stacking the books beside him on the couch. "Where did you learn so much?"

"Prison," whispered the old man. He paused. "There are better places to learn."

Before Chickie could ask more about prison, about the crimes the old man had committed, before his imagination could begin, the old man cut in, "I never did anything good in my whole life. Now maybe I can; if I can get you out, maybe I won't burn in Hell."

"Burn? You believe that stuff, Pops?"

"Yeah," said the old man, "I do."

Later, Chickie would go over every detail of those first days again and again, but he could never discover just why he decided to stay and do what the old man wanted. Maybe it was the quiet, rather ascetic existence the old man led, or the clean orderliness of the apartment that appealed to him, Chickie, whose own life had always been filled with the sounds of shouting and fights, whose mother's apartment had always been a mess. Maybe it was the surprising pleasure he felt in learning without having to dodge bullies, without the constant noise and smell of the school. Maybe it was having a friend, someone who needed him.

Chickie looked hard for answers. After all, it boiled down to a question of his own sanity. There must have been clues as to what was happening. Why hadn't he seen them?

One thing was certain: Chickie enjoyed life with the old man. He liked the housework, doing the laundry, taking showers, keeping the old man fed and clean. Gradually, Chickie came to enjoy reading aloud to the old man, came to be proud of how well he read, how he could use the words on the page and his own voice to move the old man, and himself. It was only later, much later, that Chickie realized that the old man was a natural teacher, a gifted one. The days never dragged, nothing like school, nothing like his old life at all. No, nothing. Soon the books in the apartment were not enough. The old man sent Chickie to the library with lists, then with projects.

One day Chickie arrived back late, his hair plastered with sleet. "What's the matter, Pops? You look grumpy," he grinned while he unloaded the bookbag.

"You're late."

"I got to talking with the librarian, an old guy in the research department. It was great. He's a history buff just like you. He talked to me like I was a person and not just a punk."

"Doesn't everyone talk to you that way?"

Chickie thought a minute, remembering how things had changed. The old man could barely use his right arm, just enough to write a bit and to turn the pages of a book. For a while now, the old man could sign his cheques and Chickie cashed them. He'd been scared the first time. What if somebody called the cops? But the storekeepers had been nice to him.

"Yeah," he finally replied. "Guess you're right. I don't even think about hiding from cops, social workers, or truant officers anymore."

"Sure, kid. Now you belong and you look it."

"Belong?"

"Yeah. You know, a bright kid, good student. You're just the typical middle-class kid."

"Hey, me? In your shirts and jacket, Pops."

The old guy did everything, planned a sports program for Chickie, introduced him to classical music. They even watched TV, but Chickie had to write something about every program; first it was just summaries of the plots, then critiques. The old man really worked him. Every so often the old man would get impatient, as if he had to hurry. That impatience led to their only misunderstanding.

One bitter day of a bitter week in February, Chickie splurged. He'd just had another discouraging telephone conversation with his mother, who had accused him of having found a good deal and not helping her. She'd threatened to call the cops, to declare him a runaway. The weather was down; Chickie was down, so he bought a dish of bulbs at the flower shop on the corner and carried them back under his coat.

"Look, Pops. The guy says they are paper white narcissus. They'll bloom in about four weeks, and the smell is wonderful."

Chickie loved to watch them grow and expected the old man to share his joy.

"Hey, Pops, look!" Chickie shouted when the first green appeared.

But the old man watched the growth with something like dread. Every time he looked, he'd mutter something about hurrying, about time's being nearly up. It made Chickie feel so bad to see how edgy Pops was that he nearly threw the plants out. At the last minute, he couldn't and gave the dish with the five slender green shoots to the clerk at the grocery store. That way he could still watch their progress. The old man never said a word, didn't seem to notice that they were gone.

He pushed Chickie hard on tests—timed, multiple-choice—pages and pages of them. After a while, Chickie got so that he no longer feared the tests. Soon they were even kicks. It was great to go through them, tick, tick, tick, marking the answers you knew you were expected to give. After he had mastered the system, Chickie would sometimes gripe about dumb or ambiguous questions. And for every question he asked the old man, he got a whole volume for an answer, no multiple choice there.

Then came the day when the old man told Chickie to start with the applications for schools and scholarships.

Chickie never overcame his hatred of applications. They were far worse than tests because you never knew if you'd given the right answers, you could never "beat" an application. Each one went on forever, questions, little essays, financial statements, on and on. Finally Chickie threw down the pen.

"I quit! I won't do these. Why do I need to go to a 'good school' anyway? I could get a job now. You've taught me more than any school ever could."

"Look, kid, what would you do if you didn't go to school? You couldn't get a job. You're too young. You'd be in trouble in no time. For some middle-class kids, the schools may not matter. They don't need to escape from everything a slum means. They may mess up for other reasons. You, for you, school makes a difference. We are getting you into a good high school. Now! Later on, if you have middle-class existential problems, that's life. First, we get you there."

Forewarned is forearmed, thought Chickie as he went to the kitchen to get himself a large glass of water. Thus armed, he returned.

"Okay, Pops, what's an existential problem?"

When the exam scores arrived, the old man relaxed a little. Soon after, letters came from school admissions directors requesting interviews with Chickie. The old man patted the stack.

"Looks good. We are nearly done. Good job, too."

"Pops, what about you? You can't live alone, not yet."

"Me?" The old man looked surprised. "I won't be . . . that is . . . once you've got a school, I won't mind being in an old men's home. We'll find one. Near your school. I don't give a hang for that. But one thing . . ."

"What's that, Pops?"

"I don't want to go to my grave alone. Will you promise to walk behind my casket? Crazy I know, because I didn't mind being alone, ever, but that's one thing I want."

"Sure, Pops." Chickie hastened to reassure the old man, and himself. "But you are getting stronger every day. I never thought you'd use both arms, walk a step or two. You're better. One day I'll get you outside. Spring's coming. You can smell the wet, warm asphalt."

The apartment windows were open to the spring evening air. Tomorrow Chickie would go for an interview, probably the last one, with the school the old man favored. His gift to Chickie, a tape cassette player, sat on the coffee table with five boxes of tapes beside it. Tonight the old man asked for Bach's Four Suites for Orchestra. Chickie had been reading on the couch, the old man in his chair by the window. Gradually Chickie found himself listening more and reading less until he was staring at the curtains moving in the breeze.

"Miss your friends, kid?" asked the old man.

"No," said Chickie. "I think about sending money to my ma, but one of her boyfriends would take it, or they'd drink it. And I sure don't miss having to watch out to see if one of them will decide to knock me around, don't miss the fights, yelling, mess. You'd have to be crazy to miss that. And my friends? They had the same thing, so they're mostly in the street. All they want is enough dough to cut out, but where to? Nobody has a paradise like the one we have here."

"Or me to keep you straight," laughed the old man.

Chickie laughed. "Yeah, Pops. My mom's like a kid herself. Cries when those jerks beat her, or leave her, or rip her off. Then finds another one. My sisters, all but one, are just as bad."

When he put the old man to bed, Chickie wanted very much to hug him, but he couldn't. Instead he said, "Sleep well, guardian angel." To Chickie's surprise, the old man started in shock.

"What? Oh. Yeah. G'night kid. No one ever called me that before."

"Well, maybe you never were an angel before."

"No, I guess I never was."

The school interview lasted longer than Chickie had expected. They liked him and offered him a scholarship and a summer-camp job. He was set. But it was long past lunch-time. Did Pops make it to the food he'd left for him, Chickie muttered to himself as he raced home. He was too excited, too impatient, to take the subway. He ran home, stuffing his tie into the pocket of his jacket, flinging the jacket over his shoulder, winding in and out of cars at the intersections. Pops will bust his buttons when he hears.

Into the service entrance Chickie ran, taking the stairs three at a time; no time for the elevator. Down the hall the apartment door was open, someone backing out. Guys in ambulance coats wheeling a stretcher. Another stroke, thought Chickie.

"Pops!" he cried. "What—"

"Never seen one like this," said the attendant. Then seeing Chickie's stricken face, he added lamely, "Sorry, kid."

A cop came out, still looking at his notebook.

"You knew the old man? Tough. Rent paid up, so no one had checked. But no one had seen him for months. Landlord got an order to open the door. Amazing there was no smell. Guy's been with his Maker more 'n six months for sure."

Chickie leaned against the doorjamb. Inside the apartment, the yellow light of the big, old-fashioned floor lamp lit the far end of the living room. Books everywhere.

The cop patted Chickie on the shoulder. "You just out of school for vacation? Came to see him? Your grandfather? Tough. Nobody checked on him regular? When they're this old, somebody's gotta check regular."

Chickie nodded. The ambulance attendants began to wheel the old man into the elevator. Chickie followed behind them, followed all the way so that the old man would not be alone.

About
Abner the Tinker

"Oh Abner. You fixed it. Ah . . ." Mrs. Lawson was a kind woman. She would never want to hurt Abner, and certainly not her son, Mike, who stood there flushed with success. Mike had called Abner over when the old dishwasher groaned to a halt. Then Mike helped Abner, Abner who could fix anything. Mrs. Lawson, looking vainly for the right words, struggled on. "You see, boys, the dishwasher was more than twenty years old. When it stopped, I ordered a new one. You know the kind, it prerinses and scrubs pots. I'm sorry. When you have worked so hard . . . "

Mike looked at Abner, who grinned reassuringly at Mrs. Lawson. "It's okay. Good practice for us. Well, now you can use it till the new one comes."

Mrs. Lawson was relieved. She gave the boys a snack and went about her business.

It was always the same. Somehow all the broken things found their way to Abner, who fixed them, only to learn that nobody wanted them anymore.

"Oh, this old alarm clock? Works now? Gee, thanks Abner," said Mr. Knickerbocker. "But you see, I was kinda glad when it fell off and broke. I've hated the sound of that alarm for fifteen years. Now I've got me a digital clock that says 'good morning' in fifteen languages. Here, take this one for your trouble. Maybe you can use it."

Over the years Abner got a house full of stuff, stuff he had fixed, stuff nobody wanted. He even got the house that way. By then Abner was grown up, and the house at the edge of the village had fallen down. Nobody wanted it, fine shade trees notwithstanding, so Abner got it cheap. Abner fixed it up and filled it with things he'd fixed. All the kids knew him; all the kids brought him the things they found, things that needed mending, and the kids learned a bit about fixing things from Abner. Then the kids grew up and did other things. Abner continued pretty much in the same way.

"Porcelain umbrella stand? That poison-green, chartreuse, and blue one? You mended it? Not even a seam? That's great, Abner. Say, Abner, want to keep it?" whispered Mr. Davis. "Old Aunt Hattie gave it to us as a wedding present. Antique or not, my wife hated it, and I'll admit I did, too. The day the cat knocked it over, the missus barely swept up the pieces before she ran out to buy the cat a whole kidney for dinner. So, keep it for your trouble. Maybe you can use it." He winked. "Thanks, Abner. Care for a cuppa coffee?"

Abner was no longer young when he found the broken woman. She sat every day on the same bench in the village square, holding her coat close against her with one hand, her arms around the purse that could not be closed. It was filled with packages of cigarettes. Clutching bag and coat, smoking one cigarette after another, she sat there talking furiously in a soft whisper. She seemed to be desperately clutching at herself to keep the pieces from flying away; her face, her eyes, even her hair, were drawn tight with the effort it cost her.

After the woman was mended, her face was soft, and her merry laugh made others feel happy, too. For the first time, there were many who wanted what Abner had mended. But the woman who had been broken loved Abner, and so they were married.

Children had always come around to putter with Abner, but now there seemed to be more than usual. Abner and Mrs. Abner found some broken ones, which they then mended. But where some children go, more will follow, and soon Abner and his wife had children who had been broken, children who had not, and a good number of other young visitors as well.

All this life cost money, so Abner was fortunate that Mrs. Abner had quite a few talents of her own. Where he had lived in shabby comfort, Mrs. Abner brought beauty, a way of using fabric, space, and light to make things look very nice indeed, without sacrificing comfort. She also understood more of the world than Abner did. Perhaps that was how she had come to be broken.

Into the old parlor of their house she brought all the things Abner had fixed: the umbrella stand, clocks, some old fans on pedestals—the kind that turn slowly from left to right while they run. Mrs. Abner painstakingly cleaned the fans and painted them so that they looked like bright bouquets of flowers when they stood still and gentle whirls of rainbow colors when they blew. She created a pleasant clutter, added shelves of homemade jams and pickles, and made a sign: SECONDHAND STUFF.

She was in business. People came, and to Abner's amazement, they bought. Mrs. Davis brought Mr. Davis.

"Oh, George, look. That vase with the white gladiolas in it. Isn't it beautiful? Looks like our awful old umbrella stand, but the white flowers just make it. Must be from the same period, same manufacturer, too, I'll bet. Why didn't I think of that?"

"It *is* your umbrella stand, Mrs. Davis," said Abner, coming into the shop. "You can take it. I just glued it."

"Oh, Abner," replied Mrs. Davis. "Can I? I'll pay you for the repair job. Could I have the glads, too? Thank you. George, pay Abner. What a find! Thanks!"

Abner shook his head in pleasant disbelief and went back to the repair shop in the garage. He had a car that very nearly worked.

Not many weeks later the car was fixed. The shop had done well. Abner declared a fishing trip. The children cheered, the windows rattled, and everyone ran to pack. Abner made a sign, "Gone fishing," to hang over the shop sign.

Everyone else was in the car when Mrs. Abner appeared at the screen door with the black metal cash box. "I should take this to the bank."

"Bank's closed," replied Abner.

"Oh well," Mrs. Abner said. She pushed the box under the sofa and closed the doors.

It was a great trip. A full week later they returned. Sheriff Nolting was parked in front of the house, writing on a large pad. Abner was so surprised to see him that he did not notice the house. The sheriff put down the pad when he saw Abner and walked over to their car. "Abner, Miz Abner, I'm so sorry."

Then Abner, Mrs. Abner, and the children stared in horror. The house was a mess. The front door had been pulled off, windows broken, shutters pulled down.

"Inside's worse," mumbled the sheriff. "They parked at the kitchen door. Must have come last night, late, with a truck. Cleaned out the shop and rifled the cash box, then smashed the house. You know old Miz Hewett's deaf as a post. She didn't hear a thing. Not professionals. They don't smash. By now your things are probably somewhere hundreds of miles away."

Abner said nothing. He was as close to being broken as he could be. The robbery didn't matter; the violence did. For years Abner had been protected from the world by never having anything the world wanted. Now he did. Now he, too, had become an object of envy.

Mrs. Abner, the children, and the other villagers set to work to repair the house. Abner sat. If someone said, "Hold this," he did. Otherwise Abner sat.

Abner sat for weeks. Mrs. Abner knew how to make do, so they didn't starve. It was for Abner that she needed an idea. She waited, waited and looked. The day she saw the newspaper article, she made a telephone call. Then she waited some more.

Some days later, a large manila envelope arrived in the mail. Mrs. Abner opened it. Putting the eldest child in charge of the house, Mrs. Abner put Abner into the car. Without Abner's constant attention, the car had become shaky once more. Mrs. Abner put things into the car, handed Abner the envelope, and got behind the wheel.

Abner never moved. For two hundred miles they drove in silence. Finally, just outside another little village, Mrs. Abner began to talk. Abner remained silent.

Once in the village, Mrs. Abner parked the car by a building with a small white sign. In black letters it said

"Town Hall." Going around to the side of the building, she led Abner down a flight of steps to a door marked "Basement." Abner held the folder. He had not even glanced at it. Through the door went Mrs. Abner; she felt for the light switch and flicked it. The floor of the furnace room was covered with white fragments, large and small.

"Here it is," whispered Mrs. Abner.

Abner looked. He put down the folder and bent his knees. He just crouched there and looked. Finally he picked up a piece from the floor.

"You say . . . " Abner's voice cracked; he hadn't spoken in a long time. "You say it's a statue of a Civil War vetern, hit by a car full of drunks? Knocked into lots of pieces?"

Mrs. Abner nodded. Abner rubbed his dry, callused hands on the thighs of his trousers. He picked up the envelope and opened it. Out spilled twenty-five or thirty photographs of a statue of brilliant whiteness, a statue of a Yankee soldier.

"The town wants it fixed, but no one would take the job?" Abner looked at Mrs. Abner. "No wonder. Miserable job, take forever."

His eyes were full of mischief, his face no longer slack. Abner stood up and walked over to Mrs. Abner, picking his way among the fragments. He gave her a bear hug and a loud kiss.

"They said they want to protect it once it's fixed? I have some hundred feet or so of fencing in the garage, wrought iron, same period as the statue," he said. "I can fix the missing spots of the fence. Sturdy, but won't spoil the view."

"The police chief will put you up," said Mrs. Abner. "The postmistress will let me know if you need anything. We'll miss you. First school vacation, maybe we can come and help."

"I'll need . . . " began Abner.

Mrs. Abner broke in, "I packed some tools, some glues, some clothes, too. I'll leave you the car. We can do without it for a while."

The mayor's daughter drove Mrs. Abner home. On the way, Mrs. Abner, from relief and joy, cried a little bit.

Critch

At the far end of the valley, just at the foot of the mountain, lived a witch so mean and crotchety that not a single bat, not even a black cat, would live with her. Spiders, who are the most tolerant of creatures, agreed to remain in her house only as long as she left them strictly alone.

Whenever she woke up, Critch snarled her hair, rubbed sleep into her eyes, put on her tall black hat, then her rusty, dusty, musty black gown. She clump, clump, clumped down the stairs with her shoes on the wrong feet.

In the kitchen she grumbled and complained as she got her breakfast. Her kettle never sang; her pot never bubbled merrily. All was murky gloom in the kitchen, just the way Critch liked it.

Just outside the messy courtyard of her messy cottage was a tumbledown shed, where Critch kept four sad hens. She rarely fed them, so they were thin and never laid even one egg. Critch didn't care. She got all her food through magic. At one time, long ago, she had known all her spells by heart, but now she often had to peer into her great black spell book before she could get anything to eat. No matter what the food was, Critch always complained.

A little bit past Critch's house lay a small forest. On the other side of the forest were tidy farms along a dusty road that led to a quiet village.

After her breakfast, Critch messed up her kitchen and her courtyard. Then, grumbling, she set off to work.

On Mondays she blew clouds of black soot on all the clean laundry that was hanging out to dry throughout the valley.

On Tuesdays she put knots in the wood, just where they would break the saw. Whoever was sawing wood for the fires that day would not finish in time for supper.

Critch broke many tools on Tuesdays. She broke the mill wheel so often on Tuesdays that the miller would have been disappointed if the wheel had indeed ground flour that day. He rather counted on a day spent gossiping with the blacksmith and the carpenter while they all fixed the mill wheel.

On Wednesdays, Critch made all the milk sour.

On Thursdays, she gave stomachache to all the babies, made all the children cranky, and put out all the cooking fires.

On Fridays, Critch made something different happen each week. She spent hours reading spells to find just the right thing to do for Friday. One of her favorite spells was to put incredible snarls into the hair of all the schoolchildren. As mother or big sister or big brother combed and brushed, the snarls got worse. The combing hurt; the children wriggled and cried out. Someone was sure to get a smack, and sometimes, even before breakfast, Critch could get all the children in a family crying and angry, and mothers and fathers, too. All the grandparents and old aunts and uncles nodded and said, "Yes, it's the witch. She did it when we were children, too."

After a really good hair snarling, all the children would be late for school and miserable for the better part of the day. At home, the fathers and mothers would be in a bad mood for half the morning.

On a good day, Critch cackled over her dinner and fell into bed, smiling happily, to dream of what she would do on Saturday and Sunday.

Generally on Saturday Critch stuck close to the market in the village, making fresh eggs rotten. It was wonderful to hear all the angry customers return to the egg woman, demanding their money and calling her names.

Sometimes Critch would tickle a horse so that the blacksmith got a smart kick, or make a cow run crazy among the fruits and vegetables. But best of all, she liked to call up a great windstorm to tumble all the baskets, tables, and stalls.

She blew great clouds of sand into the food. Sand got into everyone's eyes, mouths, ears, hair, and shoes. The sand stung when it hit your skin. After just half an hour of wind, everything was a mess. Market day was ruined. Critch enjoyed Saturdays.

Every Sunday, Critch tried to do something special. Sometimes she studied her spell book; sometimes she just had an inspiration. Passing the church one Sunday, Critch stopped awhile to study the peaceful scene. Everyone was inside the church. She could hear music and singing. Outside stood horses and wagons from every farm. Very quietly, she unhitched the horses and sent them home. Then, rapidly saying one spell after another, she made all the carts and wagons roll into the churchyard, then sent one wheel from each cart and wagon rolling down the hill away from the church. So many carts and wagons were jammed into the churchyard that it was nearly impossible to move. But, just to be sure that her wonderful idea would be a success, Critch said yet another spell to call into the churchyard all the carts and wagons from the village. Saying all those spells, and laughing to herself as she worked, had made Critch very tired, so she took a little nap under a bush near the churchyard while she waited for the people to come out of church.

Critch awoke, refreshed, to enjoy a splendid scene. It took them hours to find the wheels, put them back on the wagons, undo the wagon jam, bring the horses, hitch them to the wagons, and start for home. While the men and children tried to clean up the mess, the women had to walk home to make sure the dinner did not burn. For some it was a long, long walk. Critch loved the smell of burned food that hung over the valley that day. And because she wanted to provide absolutely equal misery throughout the valley, Critch herself burned all the dinners in the village and in the farms near the church.

For six hundred years or so Critch had toiled and tormented, with great success. But slowly, almost before she noticed it, things began to change. Critch had not captured a child for her dinner in years. Indeed, she could not even successfully turn a child into a toad. She tried repeatedly at the pond beside the forest, where there were plenty of round-faced children with plump pink toes. Time and again she cast her toad spell on a child she surprised playing near the pond.

"Craw, Craw, Craw," the old witched crowed, "turn that brat into a toad!" But every time, Critch screamed out with rage. Instead of a muddy brat turning into a plump green, yellow, or brown toad, Critch had turned a perfectly fine toad into yet another brat. At the sound of Critch's scream, all the children raced home.

Soon the farm families grew accustomed to these extra children. Because there was food, work, and love enough to go around, the new arrivals were welcomed, even though they looked different. Most of the farm children were blond; the "magic pond" children often had green eyes and brown or black or even red hair. Nevertheless, they ran home to supper with their new brothers and sisters and found a place to sleep in the loft, and a name as well. Meanwhile Critch stomped home to grind her stubby teeth and pore over her spell book in the smoky gloom of her kitchen.

As the years passed, more and more of Critch's spells went awry. One bright morning she decided it would be wonderful to have a flood. She wanted miles of mud, houses floating down the valley, clothes, books, and blankets ruined, the stink of rotten crops in the fields.

"M-m-m-m," Critch grinned, "it sounds delicious." Critch smacked her lips as she called her broom to take her over the forest and farms. She had pored over her spell book half the night to get the spell just right. Now she repeated it to herself as she flew, just so she would not forget it. Critch began with a spell for heavy showers. And indeed, it began to rain.

But, it did not rain water! It rained flowers.

"No!" yelled Critch, "Not flowers! Showers! Water! Mud!" But she could not change the spell. Blossoms of every color fell from sunny skies. Flowers filled the roads and farmyards. Everyone went out to see. Critch kept repeating the curse, and as she spoke, more flowers fell. The children had blossom fights. The bees made more honey than ever before. There were mountains of flowers. At first the farmers and villagers just stood scratching their whiskers, and watching. Then they got out their biggest cooking pots, sent the children to gather the flowers, and began to make gallons of sweet-smelling perfume.

While Critch sulked, the people of the valley rejoiced at their good fortune. There were quantities of honey and perfume to trade at the great market in the city. The valley had a celebration, with dances and games and prizes for everyone. Critch stayed home.

Finally, Critch flew off to see the witch doctor. "Why dearie," he crooned. "You merely need spectacles. We are all getting on in years, you know. I wear them myself."

Critch was amazed. It was all so simple. Once she got home, she went straight to her spell book and began to read with glee.

"Now I can do something special. Hm-m-m-m. Fire, flood, earthquake, perhaps a volcano in the village square. Heeeee, heeee, hee." As she read, Critch fell asleep to dream happily of all the damage she could do. But in the morning Critch discovered she had mislaid her spectacles. Try as she might, she could not find them. She tried a few spells from memory; nothing worked, not even breakfast. Her day was ruined. For weeks she grew gloomier and gloomier. Critch spent most of her time looking for her spectacles and fell behind in her work. She tried calling them with a spell, but instead of coming to her, the spectacles all too often went to the top ledge of the hen house and set the hens to clucking.

Just when she was most miserable, Critch had a marvelous piece of good luck. She was near the forest when it happened. As she was walking along, Critch stumbled. She tried to catch herself, but failed. Down she fell, onto something soft. Critch grabbed the something, then peered closely at it. Critch could not believe her eyes. It was a seven-year-old child, with long black braids. Critch had stumbled over the child asleep on the soft green grass near a blackberry patch. Holding the nasty thing by the neck, Critch stood up. Two full berry baskets were on the grass at her feet. The child's face and hands were stained with blackberry juice. Overjoyed, Critch tied up the girl, threw her over her shoulder and started for home.

Maydee, for that was the child's name, did not weep, nor struggle, nor try to cry out. She merely opened her great green eyes and looked and looked. She made Critch feel uneasy. That girl made Critch feel so uneasy that Critch nearly ate her on the spot. But Critch had a plan. Hungry as she was, Critch smiled and muttered to herself. "This farm brat can find my glasses. Then I can either fatten her up to eat, or find that spell to get myself another, more appetizing, child for supper. Once I can keep those spectacles where they belong, I can cast all my spells. Oh, everything will be dandy."

Skinny as she was, Maydee was heavy, and Critch was tired when they reached the kitchen. Critch tied a rope to the girl's neck. "Find my spectacles," she snarled in her meanest witch voice.

Maydee silently handed Critch the spectacles, which had been on the table near the big black book.

"Oh," said Critch, and put them on her long bony nose. She leaned over the book to find a spell for dinner. Before Critch could read two lines, she had fallen asleep.

Maydee, who was clever, brave, and terribly curious, immediately realized that Critch was a witch. She had listened carefully to Critch's muttering and had observed the path as they came to Critch's house. Maydee could have run home, but she did not. Instead, she took the rope from her neck and tiptoed over to Critch. Carefully, slowly, she slid the big black book from under Critch's snoring head. Quietly she crept close to the fire so that she could read. Maydee opened the book and turned the pages; her eye fell upon a spell for transporting people or things from one place to another. It was almost as if the book had turned itself to that page. Looking at

Critch, Maydee repeated the spell. Zap! Critch was gone.
Putting down the book, Maydee raced upstairs. There was
Critch, snoring loudly, completely entwined in the covers of
the messiest bed Maydee had ever seen.

Maydee returned to the kitchen, where she read spell
after spell until she became very hungry. Immediately the
pages of the book seemed to flutter in her hands, and she
found all she needed for dinner. Maydee was having such a
wonderful time that she never got even the least bit sleepy.
Finally, she put down the spell book and began to explore the
house and courtyard. She returned to the book now and then
for the spells she needed. When the sun came up, she washed
her face and hands, brushed her teeth, combed and braided her
hair, then made breakfast.

After breakfast she thought for a while; then she wrote a
letter to her mother and carried it down the hill to the road,
where she met a goatherd on his way to pasture. He promised
to give the letter to her mother that night when he returned
with the goats. Maydee had written: "Dear Mama and Papa, I
will be home in a few days. I am helping an old lady find her
glasses. Love, Maydee." Maydee crossed her fingers. It was not
exactly a lie, but . . . well, she just had to read more of that
book.

Critch awoke with a start. Sun was in her eyes. She sat up
in her bed, then got out on the wrong side, as was her custom.
She messed up her hair, then clomped down the stairs. Something was wrong. What was it?

Well, everything was wrong, that's what. In the kitchen
Critch couldn't see a thing. She squinted. Maydee handed
Critch her spectacles. Sunlight. There was bright sunlight
everywhere. The kettle was polished and sang on the hearth.
The kitchen smelled of porridge, and the table had—what?—
flowers on it. Critch was outraged and hurled her spectacles
to the floor.

"What is this mess!" she bellowed at Maydee.

"I made breakfast," said Maydee as she led Critch to the
chair. "The porridge is for me. I made some witches' food for
you, but there is porridge if you'd like to try it." She handed

Critch a cup of something hot, black, and wonderfully bitter.

"What is this?" demanded Critch.

"Coffee," said Maydee.

"Oh," said Critch.

After breakfast Critch stumbled out into the courtyard muttering, "I'll eat that girl for lunch. What a mess she has made of my cozy kitchen."

But the sight of the courtyard made Critch stop dead. "Great gobs of glop!" she yelled. "Bring my spectacles." Maydee brought the spectacles. Critch put them on and looked in amazement at the courtyard. It had a green tree in the corner, and flowers along the edge. The courtyard was neatly swept. Beneath the tree was a bench. That was not all.

"What is that racket?" screamed Critch.

"The chickens are laying eggs," said Maydee calmly.

"They should lay rabbits," snarled Critch. As she spoke six baby rabbits hopped out of the hen house. Critch looked again; the hen house was straight, tidy, perhaps even freshly painted.

"Oh, no," she moaned as she sank onto the bench. It was all too much to bear. She took off the spectacles so that she wouldn't have to see any more.

Maydee stroked a baby rabbit and looked at Critch with her great green eyes. Then Maydee put down the rabbit and went into the kitchen. The rabbit took one look at Critch, then followed Maydee.

"Go home, girl. I don't even want to eat you. I'd get indigestion," moaned Critch. "Go home. I won't even eat your little brothers and sisters. I won't have anything to do with children. Just leave me. You have ruined my house, my hen house, my courtyard," Critch wailed.

Maydee came out of the house and stood in front of her, saying nothing. Silently, she brought her hand from behind her back. Critch jumped.

"My pipe! I haven't been able to find it in years. Where was it?"

"Over the kitchen hearth," said Maydee.

"Dear old pipe," said Critch.

Like all good children in those days, Maydee knew how to clean and fill a pipe, and how to light it with a twig from the kitchen fire. Critch hated children, especially good children, but she loved her pipe. She took it, drew on it, and closed her eyes. What joy.

When she opened them, Maydee was sitting at her feet on a little stool, shelling green peas. Critch grumbled and complained. Then, slowly, she began to tell Maydee about being a witch, about the good old bad old days, about all the wicked spells, about all the mischief, about sending swarms of bees into the village to sting everyone. Critch chuckled. "That was a terrific spell. If I had my spectacles I could read it. I don't remember how it goes."

Maydee once again handed Critch the spectacles. "Oh, well, I'll just finish my pipe first," said Critch.

After the pipe Critch went inside, read in her book, then set off for the village. What a good idea she had. She would fill the village with a swarm of skunks. She chuckled and muttered to herself, "What a fine sight. What a fine smell."

Chattering and laughing, Critch approached the village and said her spell, then waited expectantly. Commotion in the village. Critch went closer for a better look. The streets were full. Full of swarms of—of—monks!

"No, no, not monks, *skunks!*" Critch wailed. She was sure she had got the spell right. It couldn't fail! Yet there were dozens of brown-robed monks, all looking bewildered, crowding the streets of the village. The people came out of their houses and shops and began to talk with the monks. The amazed villagers kindly offered the monks food and shelter until the monks could figure out where they were and how to get back home again. In exchange the monks offered to teach the villagers a secret only they knew. These monks knew how to make special, very delicious cheeses. The village was full of happy conversation. Critch was full of fury. She clenched her fists, muttered, then turned around one hundred times, spat, and clumped away dizzily toward home. She couldn't even fly.

Critch walked along the dusty road, deep in gloom. From

a distance, she heard a young man singing. A wagon approached, driven by a young farmer with a fine black moustache and sparkling blue eyes. Singing merrily, he drove his lively team of fat gray horses.

"Good afternoon, granny," he said politely to Critch.

Critch was beside herself. "Fool! Lout!" she snarled. Couldn't he see that she was a witch? He and his horses should be terrified. Critch muttered a long-forgotten curse, "Fie, fie, fie, put a cinder in your eye!" As she spoke the poor farmer pulled up his team and grabbed at his eye in excruciating pain. Tears streamed down his face, but still the cinder Critch had put into his eye hurt like fire. Satisfied, Critch walked on.

But as she turned back to gloat at the young farmer's pain, a pretty young woman came out of the courtyard of a nearby farm. In her hand was a snow-white handkerchief. Gently, she removed the cinder from the young man's eye, then led him to the courtyard, where she gave him a cool drink of water and a tender smile. Before long, the two were happily conversing. Their faces showed how glad they were to have found one another.

It was too much for Critch. She went home and sulked for days.

Maydee was helpful. Too helpful. She got Critch a pair of spectacles on a long silver chain. She sewed Critch a pocket to hold the other pair of spectacles. Still, the spells did not work as they should.

And Critch found the child so very strange.

One night after dinner Maydee took a kettle from the fire and filled a tub with warm water and sweet-smelling soap. Critch looked at Maydee with real wonder. What a mysterious child!

"What are you going to do?" she asked.

"I'm going to take a bath," said Maydee, with a smile. She looked at Critch with those great green eyes and did not blink once.

"Aug-g-gh!" shuddered Critch. "A bath! How disgusting.

That is really too much. A bath! How horrible!" Critch turned, left the kitchen, and stomped up the stairs to bed, shuddering and muttering in horror.

At first Critch yelled at Maydee all the time. She snarled and whined. Nearly every day she told Maydee what a mess Maydee had made of her cozy house, of her cozy life. "Go home," said Critch at least once a day.

But Maydee stayed.

At last Critch stopped yelling. She grew sad. She ignored the big black spell book. She did not even go to the village or to the farms. The missing spectacles and the mis-spells had discouraged her. Critch had stopped trying. She was thinking. One day she called Maydee.

"You won't leave, so I will. My spells don't work. My house is disgusting. You aren't even afraid of me. No one is afraid of me. I am leaving."

Now Maydee looked sad, which made Critch feel better. Critch went outside to smoke her pipe.

As Critch sat there smoking, a great black cloud covered the sun. A foul-smelling wind blew the dust of the courtyard into hundreds of swirls. Suddenly a black figure stood before Critch. It was Hagatha-Bagatha, one of the oldest, meanest witches of them all.

"Hagatha!" Critch shouted. "I've not seen you in three hundred years. How are you?"

"Well," said Hagatha, as she settled herself on the bench beside Critch. "I'm surprised to see you still here."

Critch grunted.

"Critch," said Hagatha, "I've been traveling for a long time now. Everywhere it is the same. Very few witches are left anywhere these days. The age of witches is past." She shook her head, then lit her pipe. "Most witches are gone. Did you know that people no longer believe in us? No one is afraid. The powers of witches are diminished or completely gone. It is a distressing state of affairs." She puffed in silence for a few minutes.

Critch nodded. "So that is what is happening. I thought it was just me. I have been miserable these last years." She told Hagatha of her mis-spells. "I'm planning to leave, myself," she concluded.

Silently, the two old witches smoked their pipes.

Suddenly, Hagatha stood up and put on her hat. "I must fly," she said.

"No!" Critch shouted. "Have some coffee. It is a wonderful, bitter witch's brew Maydee makes for me. Then stay for dinner. Maydee can cook; even though it is not real witch's food, it is good. I must warn you, though. She cannot make a bed. It is dreadful—all smooth and white. I must stomp on mine every day for twenty minutes or so to get it right before I can go to sleep. Hagatha, do stay. I haven't had witch conversation in ages. Even though your news is bad, at least now I understand what is happening. Maybe you and I can figure out something to do together."

Hagatha looked thoughtful.

"Maydee!" yelled Critch. Critch never knew where Maydee had been, but Maydee always appeared when Critch called. Except now. "Maydee! Come here!" yelled Critch once more, louder.

"Maydee?" said Hagatha. "That's a funny name for a witch."

"She's no witch," said Critch, and told Hagatha how she had captured Maydee.

"Of course, she's a witch," snapped Hagatha. "Critch, not only your eyes are bad! I saw her by the gate as I came in, and thought how lucky you are to have a little witch for company."

"But Maydee is *good*," whined Critch.

"Well," said Hagatha. "You've got to expect such things. Besides, I could tell. She is not dull and good; she is just not evil and wicked. But she is *definitely* a witch. Indeed, she may even have had something to do with your mis-spells during the time she has been with you. Some of them sound almost like jokes."

"Really?" said Critch, thinking hard. "Maydee!"

No answer. Critch went into the house.

The kitchen was dark and gloomy. There was no fire in the hearth to warm the room. Critch went back outside. The hen house was silent and tumbled down. Maydee was gone. And, she had changed everything back to the way it was before she came. Two salty tears trembled down alongside Critch's long bony nose. "She has run away."

"Come on," said Hagatha.

Critch and Hagatha flew over the farms. No Maydee. They searched the town. No Maydee.

It was after midnight when they found her, halfway up the mountain, deep in the forest, asleep beneath a tree. In her arms Maydee held a coal-black kitten, which spat and arched its back at Critch and Hagatha.

Gently, Critch touched Maydee on the arm.

The child awoke and looked at them both with her great green eyes. She stroked the kitten to calm it.

"Come home," said Critch as crossly as she could. "We are very hungry, and only you can get the right spells for dinner and coffee." Critch paused. "Please."

"Where did you get the kitten?" asked Hagatha almost kindly.

"I was lonely," said Maydee, "so I said a spell to get her."

They all flew home.

In a twinkling Maydee had the kitchen bright with light from the hearth and filled with the fine smell of dinner.

Maydee sat with her black kitten in her lap as she listened to Critch and Hagatha tell horrible, creepy, scary tales until dawn. Then the old witches went upstairs where the beds were too smooth and clean for them, so they spent some time getting things just right. Once in bed, they fell into deep, rumbling, snoring slumber.

After the two old witches had gone to sleep, Maydee whispered a few words; a tub of hot water appeared. Maydee sang softly as she took a bath.

Afterward she put on her nightgown and crept contentedly into her clean, smooth little bed. As she closed her eyes she could feel upon her forehead the soft kiss her farm mother always gave each child before it fell asleep.

Maydee awoke just as the sun peered into the courtyard. Singing to herself, she made breakfast and fed the kitten, who purred and rubbed against Maydee's legs. She tidied the kitchen. Then she and the kitten went into the courtyard with the big black book.

Maydee was reading about the plants witches use to cure sores, to make teas that stop headache, and about the plants that are good to eat, and those that are dangerous. The book seemed to be endless.

Maydee heard a traveler passing on the road. She ran out and asked him to deliver a message to her parents' farm.

It was afternoon before Critch and Hagatha awoke. "What's that noise?" they asked each other. Looking outside, they saw children playing with the black kitten in the courtyard. Slowly, holding steaming mugs of coffee and blinking in the sunlight, the two old witches emerged from the house.

Maydee introduced her brothers and sisters from the farm. Critch and Hagatha gave the children their best vinegary smiles and sat down on the bench.

"Will you please tell us some of your scary stories?" asked the children politely.

And so the years passed. Critch and Hagatha became famous far and wide for the endless, fascinating, chilling tales they could tell. They were invited to every gathering in the valley, and people came from miles away to sit in their courtyard and hear a tale or two more.

Maydee's black kitten grew into a cat, tall and muscular, who always remembered to arch his back and spit whenever the old witches came near.